PIANO ACTION
REPAIRS AND MAINTENANCE

PIANO ACTION REPAIRS AND MAINTENANCE

K. T. KENNEDY

KAYE & WARD · LONDON

A. S. BARNES AND COMPANY
South Brunswick & New York

First published in Great Britain by
Kaye & Ward Ltd
21 New Street, London EC2M 4NT
1979
First published in the USA by
A. S. Barnes & Co. Inc.
Cranbury, N.J. 08512, USA
1979

ISBN 0 7182 1205 3 (Great Britain)
ISBN 0-498-02402-4 (USA)
Library of Congress Catalog Card Number 78-75045

Set in Monotype Bembo by Gloucester Typesetting Co. Ltd
Printed and bound in Great Britain by
Biddles of Guildford

CONTENTS

UPRIGHT PIANOS

CONTENTS

CONTENTS

GRAND PIANOS

CONTENTS

FOREWORD

Piano action repairs is a skilled job which takes many years to perfect, but the following pages will give you an idea of the procedures involved.

There are so many various types and makes of pianos it is virtually impossible to cover every type individually in this book, but they are all very similar in construction and function and by reading and following this book carefully, you will be given a thorough knowledge of how to deal with the repairs and work required to bring the pianos up to a high standard. This depends, of course, on whether you have the natural ability and intelligence to enable you to handle everyday repair work, but if you have found out from your own experience on other matters that you are unable to carry out minor repairs to do with the house and in the workshop, *never* attempt any of the repair work mentioned in this book, but by all means read this book anyway and you will be given an insight into the kind of work that goes on in piano repairs.

A word about metrication: measurements in this book are given in imperial because metrication in the piano repair and regulation industry is not complete and it is hoped that, in this way, anomalies will be avoided. However for the guidance of the reader a small metric conversion table is included overleaf.

METRIC CONVERSION TABLES

Fractions of an inch		Millimetres
$\frac{1}{32}$	=	0·793
$\frac{3}{64}$	=	1·190
$\frac{1}{16}$	=	1·587
$\frac{5}{64}$	=	1·984
$\frac{3}{32}$	=	2·381
$\frac{1}{8}$	=	3·175
$\frac{5}{32}$	=	3·968
$\frac{3}{16}$	=	4·762
$\frac{7}{32}$	=	5·556
$\frac{15}{64}$	=	5·952

Fractions of an inch		Millimetres
$\frac{1}{4}$	=	6·350
$\frac{9}{32}$	=	7·143
$\frac{5}{16}$	=	7·937
$\frac{11}{32}$	=	8·730
$\frac{3}{8}$	=	9·525
$\frac{13}{32}$	=	10·318
$\frac{7}{16}$	=	11·112
$\frac{1}{2}$	=	12·700
$\frac{5}{8}$	=	15·875
$\frac{3}{4}$	=	19·050
$\frac{7}{8}$	=	22·225

1 inch	=	25·4 mm.	1 mm.	=	·039 inch
2 inches	=	50·8 mm.	2 mm.	=	·079 inch
3 inches	=	76·2 mm.	3 mm.	=	·118 inch
4 inches	=	101·6 mm.	4 mm.	=	·157 inch
5 inches	=	127·0 mm.	5 mm.	=	·197 inch
6 inches	=	152·4 mm.	6 mm.	=	·236 inch
7 inches	=	177·8 mm.	7 mm.	=	·276 inch
8 inches	=	203·2 mm.	8 mm.	=	·315 inch
9 inches	=	228·6 mm.	9 mm.	=	·354 inch
10 inches	=	254·0 mm.	10 mm.	=	·394 inch

METRIC CONVERSION TABLES

1 yd.	=	0·91 metres	1 metre	=	1·09 yd.
2 yd.	=	1·83 metres	2 metres	=	2·19 yd.
3 yd.	=	2·74 metres	3 metres	=	3·28 yd.
4 yd.	=	3·66 metres	4 metres	=	4·37 yd.
5 yd.	=	4·57 metres	5 metres	=	5·47 yd.
6 yd.	=	5·49 metres	6 metres	=	6·56 yd.
7 yd.	=	6·40 metres	7 metres	=	7·66 yd.
8 yd.	=	7·32 metres	8 metres	=	8·75 yd.
9 yd.	=	8·23 metres	9 metres	=	9·84 yd.
10 yd.	=	9·14 metres	10 metres	=	10·94 yd.

$\frac{1}{4}$ lb.	=	0·11 kg.	$\frac{1}{4}$ kg.	=	0·55 lb.
$\frac{1}{2}$ lb.	=	0·23 kg.	$\frac{1}{2}$ kg.	=	1·10 lb.
1 lb.	=	0·45 kg.	1 kg.	=	2·20 lbs.
2 lbs.	=	0·91 kg.	2 kg.	=	4·41 lbs.
3 lbs.	=	1·36 kg.	3 kg.	=	6·61 lbs.
4 lbs.	=	1·81 kg.	4 kg.	=	8·82 lbs.
5 lbs.	=	2·27 kg.	5 kg.	=	11·02 lbs.
6 lbs.	=	2·72 kg.	6 kg.	=	13·23 lbs.
7 lbs.	=	3·18 kg.	7 kg.	=	15·43 lbs.
8 lbs.	=	3·63 kg.	8 kg.	=	17·64 lbs.

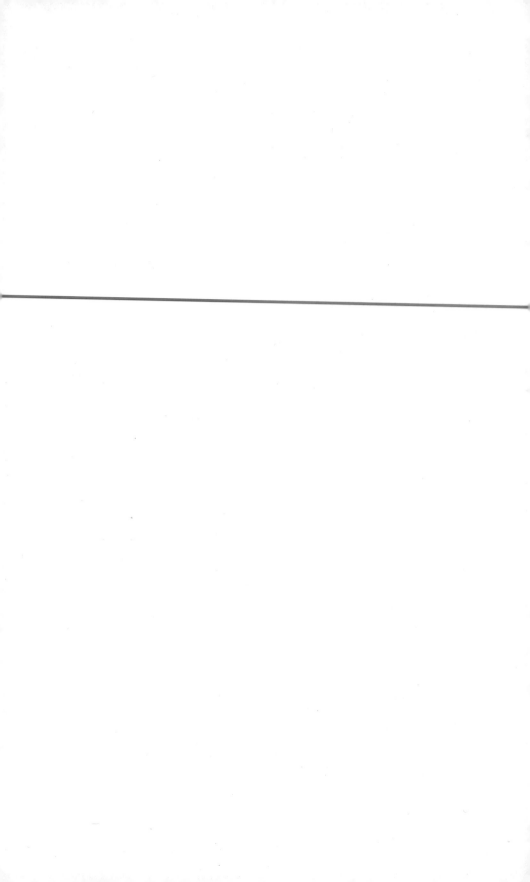

UPRIGHT PIANOS

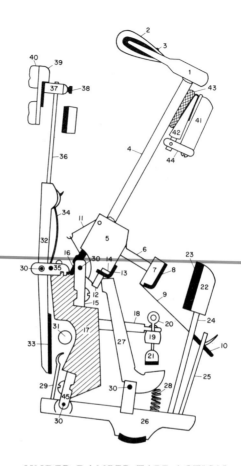

UNDER DAMPER TAPE ACTION

1. Hammer Head.
2. Hammer Head Felt.
3. Hammer Rivet.
4. Hammer Shank.
5. Butt.
6. Balance Hammer Shank.
7. Balance Hammer.
8. Balance Hammer Leather.
9. Tape.
10. Tape End.
11. Butt Spring.
12. Butt Cushion.
13. Butt Notch.
14. Butt Pad.

15. Butt Flange.
16. Butt Plate.
17. Hammer Rail Beam.
18. Set Off Stay.
19. Set Off Rail.
20. Set Off Screw.
21. Set Off Button.
22. Check.
23. Check Felt.
24. Check Wire.
25. Tape Wire.
26. Lever.
27. Jack.
28. Spiral Spring.
29. Damper Spoon.
30. Centre Pin and Bushing Cloth.

31. Damper Lift Rail.
32. Damper Body.
33. Damper Tail.
34. Damper Spring.
35. Damper Flange.
36. Damper Wire.
37. Damper Drum.
38. Damper Drum Screw.
39. Damper Head.
40. Damper Felt.
41. Hammer Rest Rail.
42. Half Blow.
43. Hammer Rest Felt.
44. Half Blow Flange.
45. Lever Flange.

UPRIGHT PIANOS

We will use a modern overstrung underdamper action as the model for repair—of course, there are many variations of actions but we shall try to cover all the main types. We will assume you have removed the action from the piano and have it standing on a work-bench with the action standing firmly supported. For the purposes of this book we will also assume that the action has to have *all* repairs carried out on it, but when dealing with work on actions one hardly ever has to cover the full range of repairs.

Now that your action is standing on your work-bench the first thing to do is un-tape all the tapes. One may be able to do this without tools but sometimes, if the tapes are tight on the tape wire, one may use pliers. Just lift up the tape end to the top of the point of tape wire and lift, turn to the left and the tape is free.

DISMANTLING LEVERS

Next, lay the action on its back with the dampers up—when the action is lying in this position make sure you have two wooden blocks, one under each end of the standards, to prevent damage to the levers. The levers must be clear of the bench. Have a tray at hand long enough to hold all the levers with room to move them along as the work on each individual lever is carried out. Now un-screw all the levers starting from the treble end put all the screws in a box and mark 'Levers'. When you reach the levers with the damper spoons use a screwdriver narrow enough not to cause hard pressure against the damper spoon, which can result in the flange breaking. It is always best to number all parts in case of accidents, because one must, when re-assembling, be sure all parts are put back in the correct order.

DISMANTLING HAMMERS

Stand the action upright, remove the screws and hammer rest. Now lay the action face down and once again place wooden blocks at each end to prevent the dampers pressing down onto the work-bench. Unscrew all the screws and place them in a small box, marking it 'Hammers' at the same time. If, when you remove the screws, you find in some instances that a screw is shorter than the rest, make a mark above the screw hole on the action beam, because the shorter screw must be screwed back into the original hole when re-assembling. You will find the screw is shorter because the damper lift rail is screwed on the other side of the beam by metal flanges and is set into the wood. Thus, if long screws are forced in it would cause damage to the damper lift flange or screw. Now, all the hammers are on a tray.

EXAMPLE OF METAL STANDARD
ON UPRIGHT ACTION

DISMANTLING DAMPERS

Stand the action up, unscrew and remove damper rail. Unscrew all the dampers starting from the treble end. Once again look out for the shorter screws and mark on the beam where they must be put back on re-assembling the action.

It is a good idea to clean the action standards and beam whilst carrying out the repairs, so if your action has metal standards and cannot be cleaned satisfactorily with a brush or other methods, unscrew the standards and depending on whether they are gold or silver in colour, apply suitable lacquer with small soft brush and allow to dry. Clean up the beam and damper lift rail with wire-wool.

RE-BUSHING DAMPER LIFT FLANGES

If the bushing on the metal or wood flanges is not satisfactory make sure to re-bush any flanges which need doing. The method of re-bushing is as follows:

If you have some of the original bushing in the flange, push this out—if it is tight apply a little methylated spirits. Flatten this bushing out to give you the width and thickness of bushing required, as there are bushings of various thicknesses. It is not necessary to use a straight edge to cut the bushing to width; make a small cut in the bushing cloth and then hold each side of the cut and pull apart. The strip will be equal all the way down. However, if it is not cut on the correct side the tear will travel out of true, so try first on a small cut to ascertain which corner is correct. When you have the bushing cloth of the correct width, cut a corner off the end to make a point. Push the point into the flange and, when the point appears, pull through until only a little more than the length needed to fill the flange can be seen. Apply a little glue and pull the bushing cloth in, cut off close to the flange and leave to dry. Fix the flange back to the damper lift rail and screw home.

17

RECOVERING DAMPERS

In the damper heads we have four types of felt, i.e. clip, wedge, split and parallel (all backed with red felt). In the bass we have clip felt for the single strings, wedge for the double strings—in which the strings are all copper covered—but over the 'break' (see note below) they are usually steel (bichord strings)—and two or three of these notes are normally damped by split felt. After this all dampers are covered with parallel felt.

Note: The term 'break' means the following: in overstrung pianos the copper strings, which are in the bass, run diagonally from top to bottom; when these copper strings end, or in fact 'break', steel strings run diagonally in the opposite direction underneath the copper strings.

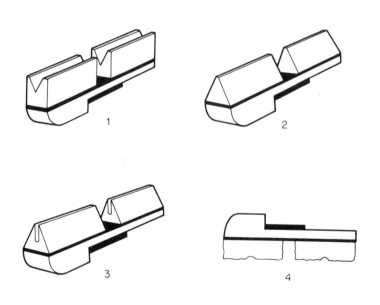

1. Clip.   2. Wedge.   3. Split Wedge.   4. Parallel.

DAMPER HEADS (UNDER DAMPER)

A sharp knife is now used to remove all damper felt from the wood, leaving the wood completely clean. If the red felt is glued so strongly to the wood making it hard to remove, first cut away the damper felt then carefully apply some methylated spirit to the remaining felt—this will make the removal of the felt easier.

Count the number of single and double strings as the dampers must be recovered with the appropriate number of felt, wedges, clip or split, e.g., if eleven singles (clip felt) are removed then replace with the same, etc. It is possible nowadays and very much simpler, to get from the Piano Suppliers the various felts already cut and backed with red felt, ready for glueing and it is advisable to buy damper felts in this way, as it saves one a lot of trouble.

For those who wish to know the other method of cutting felt you must buy one strip of wedge, one strip of clip and one strip of split. Also one strip of parallel. You will also need some red 'nameboard' felt. You will find that the damper heads in the bass are longer narrowing down towards the treble. Place the red 'nameboard' felt on your work-bench and use a good straight edge, making sure that the felt is long enough to cover right from the bass through to the treble. Pick up the first base damper, place it on the extreme left of the red felt, with the damper pressed on it, so that the top edge of the damper is almost against the edge of the felt and the bottom of the damper is against the straight edge. Then place the final treble (which, of course, is shorter) to the end of the right hand side of the felt, in the same way as before and use a sharp knife to cut along the straight edge. This leaves you with one strip of felt long in the base, narrowing down to the shorter treble.

My method of glueing the red felt to the damper head is as follows:

The best glue to use for this is Scotch glue or Pearl glue, heated in an old-fashioned type glue pot (tube glue is not suitable for this type of work). Using a small flat stick spread the hot glue carefully onto the damper wood, press the red felt gently onto the glue, making sure that one edge is flush to the underside. Press the damper hard onto the bench and using a sharp knife cut the rest of the felt cleanly away from the damper head. You may have to trim the felt slightly at the top and bottom of the damper head. Make sure you clean off any surplus glue on your knife between cuttings. Carry on recovering rest of damper heads in the same way.

We now come to glueing the actual damper felt itself. Lay a strip of 'clip' on your bench and using a piece of the original felt which has been stripped off as a pattern, cut off into pieces the appropriate lengths. Do the same with the 'wedge' and the 'split'. Now carefully glue, at the top and bottom of the felt, to the damper, always leaving a gap between felts.

The split felt, if required, is usually only needed on the first two or three dampers over the break. Fit as the originals which you have removed.

With parallel felt you may, if you wish, purchase a strip of felt which is already backed with red felt with stitching right through the middle and if you do this you may disregard glueing of red felt after the break, as mentioned above. However, before purchasing make sure you take the exact measurement of the thickness, or take a pattern piece of the old parallel felt, as the thickness of this felt can vary with each piano. Assuming you are going to use this already prepared strip of felt, you will have to make two pieces of wood, to assist you in cutting. One piece will be used as a cutting edge, the other will be an accurate method of measuring felt to be cut. The piece of wood used for giving this exact measurement (dimensions $2\frac{1}{2}'' \times 1\frac{1}{2}'' \times \frac{3}{4}''$), which we will call a 'distance piece', will have a screw ($1\frac{1}{4}$ 8) fitted into the middle of the $\frac{3}{4}''$ and this screw can be adjusted. Place this 'distance piece' flush to the side of the damper itself with the screw over the damper, turning this screw until the edge of it is exactly on the edge of the other side of the damper. Then place the distance piece close against the edge of the damper felt with the screw over the top of it. Pick up your wooden cutting edge, press this against the screw, making sure that the gap is the same all the way along.

Remove the distance piece and, still keeping the cutting edge pressed firmly onto the edge, use a very sharp knife to cut carefully this piece of felt from the main piece.

Try this piece of cut felt onto the damper to see if the cut is accurate, then continue cutting the remainder till you have enough for the job. If the first piece you cut is too wide or too narrow, discard it and adjust the screw carefully for the correct width. Once these pieces of felt are all cut correctly, glue them down to the dampers.

If this method is not used and, as mentioned before, you have covered the parallel dampers with 'nameboard' red felt, the parallel felt is cut with a space between top and bottom. Most dampers have a small space between the top and bottom and if your original dampers, which have had the felt stripped off, are like this, use the one at the break and at the treble as patterns, as they will narrow down gradually, and cut according to these. You will, of course, cut two strips exactly the same. Measure and cut as mentioned before. Glue carefully and the job is then finished.

RE-CENTRING DAMPER FLANGES AND REPLACING DAMPER SPRINGS

Remove each flange using a centre pin extractor (one that stands on the bench is best), or you may use a centre pin punch for removing old centre pins. Some people have centre pin extracting pliers, but in using these you will generally find that the pin which is pushing through the old pin gets thicker as the pressure is applied and usually the centre pin extracting pin gets lodged tight in the bushing or flange. One has to be careful to press only gently, partly in, then remove the extracting pin from the flange and pull the old pin out using ordinary pliers. Now remove all old springs from the flanges, making sure these flanges are kept in order when removed from dampers (each flange must be put back on the damper it was removed from). Damper springs can be bought from the Piano Suppliers and you will find they are of three thicknesses and will be marked bass, middle and treble (treble being the thinnest springs). Fit the new spring in place in same way as it was previously. You will find that instead of using cord to hold the spring in place, sometimes it is a good idea to just use a matchstick pushed in the hole to hold the spring. If in fact you wish to use cord to hold the spring, use a length of cord 1–2ft. The cord has an outer coating with long strands of material inside it and, by carefully pushing back the outer coating of cord and holding onto the inner strands, expose about 1″ of inner threads. You then cut these off, being careful not to cut outer coating at all, which should now be pulled back into original position making it, of course, hollow for 1″. Apply hot glue to this piece––twisting it carefully and squeezing it into a point, removing all excess glue, so that when hardened this point can be pushed through the hole to hold the spring. Pull right through to end and cut off.

RE-CENTRING

Centre pin sizes are, for general use, 23, 23½, 24, 24½, 25 and 25½, but the full range of gauges starts at 20 and goes up to 27,

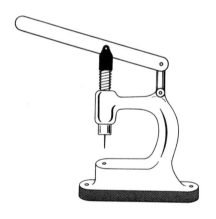

DECENTRING MACHINE   CENTRE PIN
EXTRACTING PLIERS

though these sizes are hardly ever used. It might be useful to have a centre pin gauge.

First of all pick up the 23 centre pin and try this in the wood hole, i.e. not in the bushing in the flange. If this size pushes in easily try the next $\frac{1}{2}$ size up, $23\frac{1}{2}$. Assuming this is difficult to push in by hand and you have to use your cutters to push it in, this is the size you must use. In centring, the centre pin must be tight in the wood and easy moving in the flange bushing hole. As we have decided, in this case, that size $23\frac{1}{2}$ will hold tightly in the wood, we now pick up the 23 centre pin (which is a $\frac{1}{2}$ size thinner than the pin we are going to use) and lay this onto a large, coarse file and with another coarse file apply pressure to the centre pin. By rolling the file backwards and forwards, on top of the centre pin, under hand pressure, this 23 centre pin becomes a miniature file itself. Fix this centre pin into a broachholder about $\frac{1}{8}''$ and tighten up very firmly.

Hold the broach in one hand and the flange in the other and push this broach file into the bushing hole, turning gently. Now pick up the $23\frac{1}{2}$ centre pin, try this in the flange bushing hole and you should find that this centre pin fits easily. Now you are ready to insert this new centre pin to hold the flange and damper together. You do this by holding your recentring cutters in one hand and placing the centre pin in the cutters as near to the end as possible. Now insert the pointed end of the centre pin into the bushing hole and, using a slight twisting motion of the hand, work the centre pin through, so that the pointed end can be seen at the other side of the flange. Sometimes the centre pin is very difficult to get into the wood, despite being the right size and it might be advisable to use a pad of hammer or engineering felt, very thinly coated with grease to which the centre pin should be gently applied. This will help the centre pin to be pushed into the hole. Now hold the damper and try the flange for free movement. If this is satisfactory, cut the centre pin off close at each side of the flange.

In nearly every case, when fitting new damper springs, you will find the damper spring itself is too long. If the damper spring you have just recentred is too long, bend the damper wire level with the centre of the damper lever punching (this is a small piece of circular felt fitted in a groove). Then snip off extra length not required. Do this to all the dampers and this job is now complete.

RECOVERING DAMPER TAILS

Damper tails are covered in several different ways, the simplest being is when they are covered in boxcloth. If your damper tails are, in fact, covered in boxcloth make sure you recover them with exactly the same thickness as before, as the thicknesses can vary. When you have removed the old boxcloth from the damper tail you will keep and use one piece as a pattern to work from. Cut off a strip exactly the same as the longest piece of your pattern. Now you have to cut individual narrow pieces which will be glued back onto the damper tail. The method of cutting these narrow strips is to use a cutting block, which you can make from a piece of wood. This cutting block is very simple to make and you will always find this useful when doing similar work. It consists of one piece of wood, 2″, the way the grain is running, by $1\frac{1}{4}″ \times \frac{3}{4}″$ high. Measure exactly the width of the wooden damper tail and if this happens to be, as an example, $\frac{1}{4}″$, measure this from the edge inwards and carefully chisel out a groove about $\frac{1}{8}″$ deep, first making a straight cut with your saw.

Lay the long strip of boxcloth, which you have cut to the measurement of your pattern, on your bench and using your cutting block, press gently onto the felt so that the felt is stopped by the groove underneath the block. Now use a sharp knife to cut close to the edge of the cutting block. I must point out that the $\frac{1}{4}″$ mentioned is only an example and may or may not be the width of your damper tail. Your rule will give you the guidance to the correct measurement to use when making your cutting block.

If your damper tails have boxcloth and a covering of leather, cut leather as before with boxcloth, using your old piece of leather as a pattern for correct width and length. Glue this over the boxcloth on your damper tail as before. It is advisable when glueing leather onto the damper tails to do the glueing in two parts. First glue the strip of leather to the bottom of the damper tail (usually there is a groove for this to fit). When the glue is set you can now bend the longer length of leather around the tail covering the boxcloth underneath. This leather usually extends a little beyond the boxcloth and is glued to the wood as well as to the end of the boxcloth.

REPAIRS TO HAMMERS

By hammers, in this context, we mean everything to do with the hammer head itself—shank, butt, balance hammer, butt flange etc.

We now have the hammers, which have been dismantled from the action, on a suitable tray. First we will remove all the flanges. If the butt has a metal butt plate which holds the flange, you just turn up the butt plate screw which enables the centre pin, which is still on the flange, to slide out. This done, gently turn back the screw to hold the butt plate firmly. If your butt has no metal butt plate but is solely made of wood, remove the centre pin as explained in the removal in dampers. Next, assuming that everything has to be done to the butts because of moth or wear etc., we remove the cushions, notches and pads. Whilst we are doing this we shall also remove the tapes and the leather from the balance hammers, leaving one tape on a butt as a pattern for reference.

In some cases there are no butt springs, but we shall assume here that there are butt springs to be removed. There are two ways in which they are fitted. One is fitted by having two very thin holes drilled in the butt itself to hold the spring, in which the tail of the spring is pushed through the hole then out through the next hole to hold the spring. The tail, which should be longer, will then be snipped off close. The more usual way, nowadays, is to have a hole right the way through the butt and a cord or piece of wood pushed through to hold the spring in place.

RECOVERING NOTCHES, CUSHIONS AND PADS

We shall now start recovering the notches, cushions and pads. The pads are of various thicknesses, depending on the type of butts you are repairing. So you must ensure you have them exactly the same as the ones you have removed. These pads are made of thin boxcloth or bushing cloth. You must also have suitable leather of the same thickness as that previously removed. Also, you will find that the cushions have various thicknesses, so one must again make sure one has the correct thickness as before.

For speed in the Trade we recover these in groups of five or six. So place five butts closely together using thin string to tighten together on the shanks. Now glue your long strip of pad, using

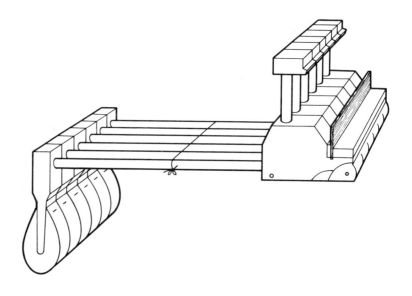

EXAMPLE OF HAMMERS TIED TOGETHER AT THE
SHANKS TO RECOVER NOTCHES, CUSHIONS AND PADS

your measurements as on your butts, e.g. measurement of pad fitted to one butt can be $\frac{1}{4}'' \times \frac{5}{16}''$, but for one strip it should be $\frac{1}{4}'' \times$ just over $2''$ to allow for trimming at both ends. Measure the notch leather which can be, for example, $\frac{11}{16}'' \times$ the length of $2''$ (as before, doing five in a batch), but always check your own measurements.

Having glued your pad we now continue by glueing the notch leather. Using a glue stick apply glue to lower part or groove of the pad. Press leather down firmly into position. You may find a knife useful to push the leather into the groove, which is usually there.

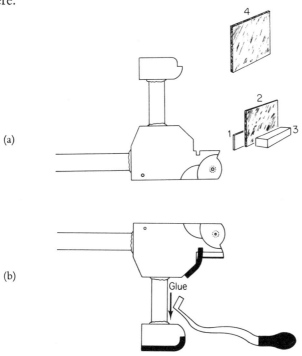

(a)

(b)

1. Pad.   2. Notch Leather.   3. Cushion.   4. Balance Hammer Leather.

(a) THE BUTT
(b) GLUEING TAPE IN PLACE

27

Next apply the glue carefully along the front for glueing the cushion strip in place, ensuring that no glue whatsoever reaches the leather itself. This will leave a piece of the leather not yet glued down, but carry on as above, throughout the whole set. Now the glue on the first five butts, which you started on, will have hardened enough to enable you to glue the rest of the leather down. When all glueings are firmly set, use a very sharp knife to trim each end of each set of five butts first of all and then, carefully placing knife between each butt, cut down and separate.

RECOVERING BALANCE HAMMERS

Cut strips of leather $1'' \times$ whatever the length may be. Although you can recover balance hammers in groups of five, as with notches and cushions, you might find it easier to recover these individually.

Recover in sets of five

As before, tie five of the hammers together at the shanks. You have already cut the strips of leather into $1''$ plus the length. Now cut into $2''$ lengths. Therefore, it will be $1'' \times 2''$. First glue on the narrow part of the balance hammer, along the ridge, and press this firmly down. Do this to each group of five. Then, when all the sets of five have been glued in this way, you are now ready to glue the longest part of the leather to the balance hammer. You may find this longer piece of leather tends to come away from the glueing slightly, unless it has some pressure or weight applied to it. Complete glueing throughout the set and when the glueing is hard you will be able to cut and separate each balance hammer and trim off any excess leather.

Recovering individually—Butts and Balance Hammers

As before in damper tails, we suggest you make a cutting block to aid you in cutting individual strips accurately. For this purpose we suggest you use a piece of wood, $1\frac{1}{2}''\times1''$ (the way of the grain) $\times\frac{4}{5}''$ and channel out a groove, $\frac{5}{16}''\times\frac{1}{16}''$ deep. ($\frac{5}{16}''$ is an approximate measurement as the butts can vary slightly, so always use your own measurements).

Cut your pads into individual strips of $\frac{1}{4}''\times\frac{5}{16}''$. Then cut your leather into strips of $\frac{11}{16}''$. Now use your $\frac{5}{16}''$ cutting block to cut pieces from this strip and your leather should now be $\frac{11}{16}''\times\frac{5}{16}''$. Pick up one butt and glue one piece of pad into position. Next glue one piece of leather onto the pad. Then cut a strip of cushion felt using the measurement of your butt—this can be, for example, $\frac{1}{4}''$. Use your $\frac{5}{16}''$ cutting block to cut your pieces of cushion felt into individual pieces. Glue this cushion in position, making sure no glue gets onto the leather notch. When you have done all this to each butt of the set, you can then finish the glueing of the leather notch.

THE IMPORTANCE OF A CUTTING-BOARD

Although not mentioned before, it is essential to have a good cutting-board (about $9''\times2'$) for all your cutting purposes, in order to protect your bench.

TAPES

Tapes can be fitted in two ways: on the balance hammer itself or on the butt near the balance hammer shank, whichever way the manufacturers have chosen. When the tapes are fitted new they are inserted and glued with the actual balance hammer shank itself, but in replacing the tapes we do not do it in this way at all.

As mentioned before, when removing the tapes you should have left one on the butt or balance hammer as a pattern. You can remove this by cutting very close to the butt or balance hammer shank, which will give you the exact length of tape required. You now tap a centre pin, maybe a 24, into your cutting-board showing about $\frac{1}{4}$". Now press the tape hole into the centre pin and smooth the tape itself out straight and mark the length on your board with a pen or pencil. Now make another mark from this first mark of $\frac{1}{8}$". You are now going to cut your tapes to this measurement (including the extended $\frac{1}{8}$"). When purchasing sets of tapes you will always find the tapes are longer than necessary, which enables you to cut the length you require.

Now we are ready to glue the tapes into position. First we deal with glueing to the balance hammers. As mentioned before, it is best to use the old-fashioned type glue in a glue-pot using Scotch, Beed or Pearl glue. Bend the extended $\frac{1}{8}$" of the tape over and put some glue on the balance hammer and slightly up the shank as well; press the tape onto this, making sure the extended $\frac{1}{8}$" of the tape is glued onto the shank. Now put extra glue over this tape and also slightly touching around the shank. This should give an extremely strong glueing.

The method of glueing the tapes onto the butts is very similar. Between the notch and the shank there is usually a gap of about $\frac{1}{8}$". Apply the glue to this space on the wood. The tape is pressed into position making sure the bent over $\frac{1}{8}$" of extra tape is facing towards the notch. The longer piece of tape will be nearest to the shank. Now apply a second coat of glue, this time on top of the $\frac{1}{8}$" extended bit of tape and once again slightly touching around the shank.

Before glueing make sure the tape is facing the correct way round, i.e. the tape end is facing correctly.

If it is unnecessary to do a complete set of tapes and only tape ends are required, first make sure all the old tape ends are removed from the original tapes. Lay the butt on your bench. Once again you must have a centre pin knocked into your cutting-board, showing about $\frac{1}{4}$". Now push the tape hole onto this pin, pick up your new tape end, cover this with glue and press the tape end hole firmly onto the pin and with a knife press the tape end firmly down onto the tape. To remove this place the knife underneath the tape and lift it off the pin carefully.

RE-FACING HAMMERS

When hammers have been playing over many years the nose gradually develops indentations through striking the strings and, sometimes, if centres have side play or there is a slightly loose screw in the flange, one has to re-face the hammers to give them a new lease of life. Usually it is possible to re-face hammers but, sometimes, if the hammer felt is worn so that the wood is showing through the felt on the nose (usually in the treble), or if the hammers are hard or generally not suitable anymore, the hammers must be recovered. However, we cannot deal with this in this book as this requires special equipment which is very expensive, and it is best if you need them recovered to send them to the firms giving this type of service.

Assuming your hammers are suitable for re-facing one goes about it as follows:

It is best when re-facing to have no flanges on the butts at all or if, for any reason, you do not wish to remove all your flanges it is possible to remove every third flange from the treble to the break and every second flange from the bass area. The reason for this is when we re-face hammers we usually deal with groups of ten at a time held closely together with string tied tightly around the shanks and if the flanges were not all removed (or as suggested above, every third and second), there would be a fanning out effect from the hammers to the butts, making them very awkward to handle.

Assuming that the flanges have been removed, start in the treble, taking the first ten and tying them tightly together with the hammers carefully placed together. Place the wooden part of the hammer in the vice with the hammer felt protruding away from it. First brush off all dirt and dust from hammer felt. Use medium sandpaper and a sandpapering block and gently sandpaper away the remaining surface of dirty felt from the wooden end (where the pin is), towards the nose. The idea is to make the nose pear shaped. Whatever you do, do not try to take away too much felt from the nose, but work from underneath towards the nose and on top towards the nose. Next apply white chalk to the felt area and using fine sandpaper repeat the above, but this time you are working in the chalk and finishing off the sandpapering giving a new appearance to the felt. When the nose of the felt is correctly pear shaped brush off all surplus chalk.

Note: It is not absolutely necessary for you to remove the indentations on the noses of the hammers, but just give them a pear shaped surface.

While the hammers are in the vice it is possible to sandpaper the surface of the wood on the hammers, but of course, if your hammers have been previously varnished or French Polished, it will only be necessary to wipe them with a damp rag.

Re-face the remaining hammers in the same way. When completed make sure you dust away all surplus chalk from between and at the sides of the hammers. Re-facing hammers is a very specialised job and great care should be taken in doing this work.

If you have an action which needs nothing doing to it at all except for re-facing hammers, it is possible to reface them without dismantling anything. All you need is a long strip of wood long enough to go the length of the hammers, i.e. to fit just inside the standards to reach from the extreme bass to the extreme treble. This wood need only be $\frac{1}{4}''$ thick by $\frac{1}{2}''$ and should be under the hammer heads, along the shanks and tied with string at frequent intervals around the wood between the shanks and then around the hammer rests and then knotted. This prevents the hammers coming away from the hammer rests whilst re-facing. Re-face as before but, of course, the hammers will still keep their natural spaces between.

FITTING NEW BUTT SPRINGS

There are mainly two lengths used in butt springs—$\frac{7}{8}''$ and $1''$, but sometimes you do get $\frac{3}{4}''$. There are left or right hand tails. I must point out, when purchasing your butt springs to be sure to get the springs with the tail on the correct side, i.e. left or right, because if you have it on the wrong side it will be impossible to fit the springs. In some cases the holes drilled for the butt springs are drilled on the left and in other butts you may find they are drilled on the right.

Example: When ordering—$\frac{7}{8}''$ Left or $\frac{7}{8}''$ Right.

You will know what length your springs are when you remove the old ones and measure them. If your butt has two holes on the side for inserting the butt spring wire, you merely insert the long wire until the coil is in the groove on the butt, then with this pulled down, push the extended end through the other hole, pull tight and with cutters snip off close to the butt. The other method of fitting butt springs is when there is a hole drilled right through the butt and there is a groove of $\frac{1}{16}''$ in the butt itself where the spring fits. This can be fitted with cord as mentioned previously on damper springs, or thin matchstick or similar type of wood.

RE-FITTING LOOPS TO FLANGES

In many cases odd loops break and you need the special loop cord for replacing these. Remove the old loop and use a small saw to open the grooves to enable you to put the new loop in place. One method to put the replacement loop in accurately is as follows:

First place your flange on your bench and knock two centre pins into the bench, flush with the top of the flange, in the inside of the

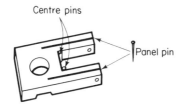

Centre pins

Panel pin

FITTING LOOP TO FLANGE

corners of the flange. Knock a third pin, maybe a 1″ panel pin (you must get a flange with the loop already fitted, which will give you the correct length), at the top on the inside of the loop, right in the middle. This pin must be ½″ above the level of the flange. Place the flange to be re-looped in position and apply glue along the grooves. Put the loop in one side, pushing down firmly into the groove, then round the top panel pin and then press the end into the groove on the other side. Trim with a sharp knife and remove flange. Using this method you will always have a loop of exactly the same length each time you do one.

RE-BUSHING FLANGES

Sometimes you may have to re-bush a flange. If one side of the bushing is out you must also push out the other side. If this is difficult a little touch of methylated spirits applied to the bushing will make the removal of the bushing easy. When ordering your bushing cloth ask for 'bushing cloth for bushing flanges', as there are various thicknesses. You will find that if you tear your bushing cloth the correct way it will tear accurately right the way down; if torn the incorrect way the tear will widen. To test this cut ¼″ with a knife into the bushing cloth and by tearing apart you will find which is the correct side, i.e. if the strip measures ¼″ all the way along. Once you have decided on this you are ready to tear off the strips of bushing cloth for your use. Make a cut ⅜″ from the end with your knife at this point and tear off your strip of bushing.

To use the bushing cloth you will have to make a point at one end, i.e. cut a point from left to right, about 1″ long. Now prepare your bench. Rub some chalk on part of your bench, about 4″ × 1″. Dip the point of the bushing cloth into your hot glue, remove excess glue with your fingers or with a rag. Before the glued point is hardened twist it around in your fingers, then place this pointed and twisted end on the chalked bench and with a flat piece of wood roll the point. The chalk clings to the point giving it a light coating, there by stopping it from sticking to the bench. This point, when hardened, should make it possible for you to push it into the bushing hole on the flange and out the other side. Pull further through carefully with your fingers until the flange has reached within 3″ of the length of bushing. If you have a lot of re-bushing to be done, you may put more flanges on the strip, each close to the next. The 3″ of bushing cloth extending beyond the first flange should be placed in a vice, about ¼″, to hold the bushing. Apply the glue to the top of the bushing and slide the flange along to the end. Do this with each one. When the glue is set cut in between each flange and cut the centre piece in the middle of the flange out as well.

Note: When re-centring a flange which has been re-bushed, you must only use a long, smooth broach, not as a file as previously mentioned in recentring, e.g. if the centre pin to be used is a 24, use a 25 long, smooth broach fitted in a broachholder. The reason for this is that the new bushing will be much softer than bushing which has been in the piano for many years. These long, smooth broaches may be purchased from Pianoforte Suppliers.

RE-CENTRING HAMMER FLANGES

We will start by describing the method by which you re-centre hammers which have butt plates attached to the butts. Re-centring of hammers is usually necessary because the centre pin is tight in the bushing. This is probably caused by a piano not being played for many years. *Warning*—you must never put oil on the hammer flanges. Centre pins were, for a long time, made of brass which, over many years, undergoes an ageing process and begins to expand slightly and crack up.

As mentioned previously, you should have already removed the flanges. Now remove the centre pins. This is easily done when the flanges have been held by butt plates, by sliding the centre pin out with your cutters. As before, you must determine what gauge centre pin you are going to use. First try your thinnest centre pin, a 23, in the bushing of the flange. If this goes in and is too loose try the next size. Usually you do not have to broach flanges held by butt flanges because you are removing an old 24 centre pin (for example), which has become tight and replacing it with a new 24 centre pin. Assuming you find that the 24 centre pin goes into the bushing easily with no side or lifting movement, then once again, if you put your centre pin onto your grease pad (this grease should not be in excess), push the centre pin in until the blunt edge is flush with the flange and the pointed end is extended beyond the other side of the flange. With your small screwdriver open up the butt plate by turning the screw out slightly and under the butt plate you will find a groove for holding the centre pin. Make sure the centre pin is in this groove before you tighten up the screw on the butt plate and, as you are using a flange with a loop, loop this to the butt spring. The flange must now have free movement to enable the hammer to operate. It is advisable to put

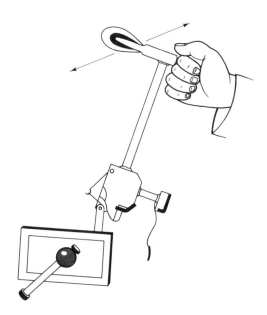

TRYING FOR SIDE-PLAY

the flange in a vice and put your thumb on top of the hammer near the shank and try for side play. If this has no side play then cut the extended centre pin close. If there is side play then you must put the next size centre pin in. It is important that there must be no side play whatsoever in hammers that have been re-centred, but only its natural movement as a flange.

RE-CENTRING WHERE THERE
IS NO BUTT PLATE

In this case the hole for the centre pin must be tried in the butt itself *not* in the flange bushing as before in butt plate centring. For example, if the old centre pin was a 24, unlike with butt plates another 24 would be too loose in the wood and the next $\frac{1}{2}$ size would have to be used. Once again, try with maybe a 23 centre pin or a $23\frac{1}{2}$ etc. The centre pin must always be tight in the wood. So that if the $23\frac{1}{2}$ centre pin pushes into the hole easily and a 24 is tight to get in, you must use a 24. If you decide that the 24 centre pin is the size you are going to use, just take a pin of the size below, which in this case will be the $23\frac{1}{2}$, place this pin on top of your file (as mentioned in re-centring dampers) and with another file placed on top of the centre pin give a hard rolling movement to the pin. This makes this centre pin into a miniature file. Fix this centre pin into your broachholder. Broach your first flange with the same —you will find that in fact it will file out some of the bushing that is in the flange. Next, pick up your 24 centre pin and apply it sparingly to your grease pad and try the centre pin in the bushing in the flange. If this enters easily with no hard pushing necessary, remove the pin, apply the flange to the butt and holding the centre pin on the extreme end with your cutters, with a slight twisting movement insert the pin into the flange bushing, through the butt hole out the other side of the flange. Try for side play—if there is none and the flange moves easily, all is in order so loop up to the butt spring. Cut off the centre pin closely, with your cutters, on each side of the flange. One point to mention is when you are working the centre pin into position, hold the butt and not the flange with your other hand.

LEVERS

Take out all the centre pins on the flanges and jacks, keeping them in correct order, and remove spiral springs—in some cases spiral springs lift out easily, but sometimes they are glued into the levers and you have to remove them with pliers. As before we are going to assume that everything needs to be done to the action. You must strip off the check felt from the checks. Keep one piece of check felt and one spiral spring as patterns. Spiral springs are in various sizes, the most used being $\frac{5}{8}''$, $\frac{3}{4}''$, $\frac{7}{8}''$ and $1''$. When replacing spiral springs the new ones must be exactly the same length as before. Usually spiral springs last for many years. Also, check felt has a very long life, unless the leather on the balance hammer wears through to the wood—when this happens the check soon wears through as well.

Re-centre flanges as mentioned before in dampers and hammers, making sure, of course that you have chosen the correct gauge centre pin. Do the same also with the jacks. Fit new spiral springs, the same size as before, without glueing unless, of course, the springs you removed were glued. In most cases the reason for the glueing is that if the lever were un-taped or removed, because of the way the lever is made, the jack can fall right back and the spiral spring would fall away if it was not glued. But in other actions the jack only moves back a certain distance so the spiral spring is held quite safely in position.

RECOVERING CHECKS

You will find that most checks are covered with $\frac{1}{4}''$ check felt, but make sure you get the exact thickness of check felt previously used. Cut a length of this felt to your check measurement (usually about $1''$). It is best to use a cutting block as mentioned before and

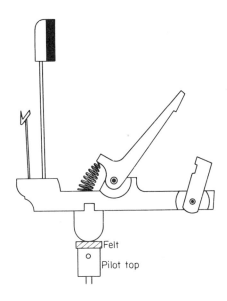

LEVER BOTTOM WOOD BLACK LEADED

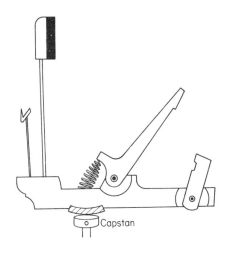

LEVER BOTTOM FELT COVERING

39

cut pieces accordingly—usually about $\frac{5}{16}$". Glue individually.

Also underneath the lever we have thick boxcloth which rests (when in the piano) on the capstan (pilot) screws. In most cases this boxcloth is green and is $\frac{1}{8}$" thick. Cut a strip (measuring the boxcloth you have removed—it could be $\frac{3}{4}$") and use your cutting block to cut each piece and then glue.

SET OFF (ESCAPEMENT) REGULATING SCREWS

Sometimes these screws, through rust, become extremely tight and if you try to force them with your set off screwdriver, the head easily breaks off. To cure this you must unscrew and remove the set off rail from the action. This may be in one long rail or two or three separate rails. Apply heat to the set off screw tops using your casting lamp or something similar. This causes heat to travel through the metal expanding it slightly. When this has got cooler, contracting again, carefully try your set off screwdriver to satisfy yourself that there is free movement. Go through all the screws in the same manner. If you find that some of the heads of the screws have already broken off, these must be replaced. The wooden set off button underneath must be removed and if the remainder of the set off screw is rusted in, also apply heat to this, using pliers when cool to unscrew carefully and replace. Set offs must all have free movement for accurate regulation.

JACK SLAP RAIL

If this needs recovering, recover with the same thickness cushion felt.

BURNISHING

On the jacks you must black lead the parts which have been done previously. Sometimes the underneath of the lever is black leaded rather than covered with felt. Apply here also. There is a new material which can be used instead of black lead and if you use this you do not have to burnish. To burnish black lead all one does is use a brush or a piece of hard felt, such as check, and rub this over the black leaded areas. This should give a good shine.

RE-ASSEMBLING DAMPERS

Now all the repairs have been completed on dampers, hammers and levers, we are ready to re-assemble the action. The first thing to assemble will be the dampers—start with screwing the first treble in place and working down to the bass. When the dampers are screwed onto the beam fit the action into the piano. One must always do this as everything in the action has been taken down and all felts changed and there will be slight differences in the way it is set up. We must now make sure that the spacing of the dampers is correct. From the treble to the break there are three steel strings for each note and after the break the bichords and finally the singles (copper covered). Using your damper spacer make sure that the dampers are correctly in line with the strings. When spacing is correct (your eye should tell you this), the most important thing is that the dampers do their job correctly, i.e. damp and lift off evenly when the loud pedal is applied (some-times called sustaining).

To achieve this adjust the pedals so that the loud stick is just lifting the damper lift rail, but not in fact lifting the dampers off the strings themselves. This adjustment is on the nut above the pedal on the rocker. Of course, to get to this you must remove the bottom door of the piano. By applying your foot to the loud pedal all the dampers must lift off the strings together. You may find that some of the dampers are slower than the rest in coming away from the strings, in which case you must crank them away a little, so that they lift together with the other dampers. If some dampers come away too soon crank forwards towards the strings. All this work on spacing or cranking forwards or backwards is done on the damper wire. This may seem a tedious job, but it is very important that dampers all lift together—so time spent on this operation is never wasted. Apply pressure to the loud pedal bringing all the dampers off the strings and this done, run your finger from the bass to the treble, along the strings, making all the notes sound. Then lift your foot off the pedal so the dampers return to strings, but if any of the notes are still sounding—there may be one or two like this—they might not be in alignment with the strings or need some other adjustment. When you are satisfied that all dampers work well, re-fit damper rail—this, of course, you may recover if required. This is a straight-forward job and requires the same felt that was used before.

RE-ASSEMBLING HAMMERS

Assembling of hammers can be done whilst the action is in the piano and we will adopt this method, although some people assemble them on the bench. Start from the first treble, screw the hammer home making sure the hammer is striking the string correctly, then move to the next hammer, right through to the last bass. If necessary recover the hammer rest before screwing onto action. This is a very simple job—just remove hammer rest felt from the half blow, using a chisel if this is required. Also remove, if necessary, the name board felt which covers the half blow. Just cut a piece of name board felt as required, recover as before and, next, glue on hammer rest felt—this may be obtained in a ready cut strip from Piano Suppliers. Now the hammer rest is screwed onto the action one must make sure that the hammers are well spaced, striking the strings correctly. Sometimes you may find that when you push a few of the hammers together towards the strings, instead of the hammers travelling together keeping the same spacing between each one, a hammer may travel to the left or the right, sometimes nearly touching the next hammer. To make the hammer travel true if, for example, the hammer is bearing to the left all you need to do is to unscrew the butt screw slightly and insert a small, thin piece of paper, $\frac{1}{16}'' \times \frac{1}{2}''$, on the left-hand side between the flange and the beam. You may find it necessary to use sticky paper for this and remove butt and flange completely, then wetting the sticky side of the thin bit of paper, press it till it sticks to the flange. Now replace butt and flange, screwing home well to the beam. If, of course, the hammer travels to the right you deal with it in the same manner, but on the right side.

CASTING LAMP

When you have reassembled hammers you may find that the hammers twist to the right or left and need squaring up. To do this we use a casting lamp, which should have methylated spirits in it. If the hammer is twisted to the right, light the casting lamp and, holding the hammer head in your other hand bringing the hammer forward off the hammer rest, very carefully apply the lighted casting lamp to the shank itself, moving this up and down along the shank twisting the hammer carefully to the left (not in excess).

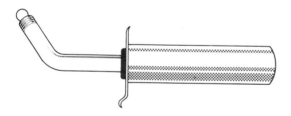

CASTING LAMP

Important: The casting lamp should only be applied for a few seconds. You must make certain that nothing catches alight, as this is very easy to do if you are not careful.

When you release your hand from the hammer, you will find that the twist will have been corrected. But you may have to repeat this process a few times if it has not twisted correctly. Of course, hammers twisting to the left must be dealt with in a similar manner. All hammers must now be evenly spaced travelling to the strings correctly. When you feel this is to your satisfaction, this completes the procedure.

RE-ASSEMBLING LEVERS

You must re-assemble levers on your bench. Lay the action down, with the hammer rest on the bench and the dampers facing up, but place wooden blocks under the standards at each end (treble and bass) to raise the action about 1″ or so off the bench. Starting from the treble place the first lever in position and screw down, making sure that the jack is not between the set off (escapement) rail and jack slap rail. Continue through the action until completed. In some pianos some of the jacks have cut out spaces to make room for the rail brackets for set off rail and jack slap rail. Make sure these are in the correct position, but other modern actions have these spaces cut out of all the jacks.

Stand the action up on the bench. You now tape up tapes to tape wires. Sometimes the holes in the tape ends might need opening to tape up easily. This you can do with a bradawl, being careful not to make the hole too wide, as this might damage the tape end. Now you turn the action upside down, ensuring that the hammers do not touch the bench, which can be achieved by placing blocks under the standards. To prevent accidents, it is also best to cramp on the treble standard to prevent the action falling. You must have the action in a position so that the lever screws are towards you. The idea of this is to look down between the levers to see that the jacks are correctly in place on the notch and cushion, i.e. in alignment with them. If it is necessary to square up, one only has to release the screw slightly and adjust the lever on the notch to correct position. Go through the action until all are correct. If you cannot manoeuvre in the way mentioned because when screws are tightened up the Jack returns into the wrong position again, i.e. too far to the left or right of the notch—use paper as

44

mentioned before in hammers, about $\frac{1}{16}'' \times 1''$, inserting between the flange and the beam to the right if the jack is to go to the right or to the left if the jack should go to the left. Tighten up the screws.

When all this is completed stand the action in an upright position on the bench. Now you must adjust the tapes so that the jacks will have a little movement between the jack and the notch, about $\frac{1}{16}''$. This will enable the jack to operate properly when played. If the space is more than $\frac{1}{16}''$, i.e. $\frac{1}{8}''$ or more, this must be corrected by pulling the tape wire towards you (this will remain in the position), or if the jack is tight on the notch, carefully push the tape wire in slightly, giving you the necessary space required. This is important for correct movement. You may find that the checks, here and there, are not squarely spaced to the balance hammers. This can be corrected by using your check bender.

CLEANING KEYS

Before fitting the action once again into the piano, we must remove the keys from the piano. Place them on a suitable board to keep them in correct order. If you want your keys cleaned you must use a machine with a buffing wheel and buffing soap, but if you do not wish to do it yourself, you may send the keys to the key specialists, who will scrape and polish your keys for you. If you have ivory keys and they are very discoloured the professional firm will do an excellent job for you, but if you want to do the work yourself, here is the procedure:

This is for *ivory keys only*. You must have a sandpapering block, also some medium and fine sandpaper. First use the medium sandpaper. With your key flat on your bench, place the sandpaper and block firmly onto the key and rub with good firm pressure until the discoloration has gone. Next use your fine sandpaper to get rid of any scratches. Go through all your naturals in this fashion. *Do not use this method on your sharps.* You finish this on your buffing wheel, using only a little buffing soap on the wheel.

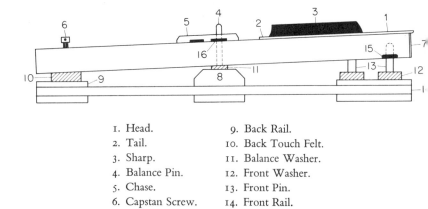

1. Head.	9. Back Rail.
2. Tail.	10. Back Touch Felt.
3. Sharp.	11. Balance Washer.
4. Balance Pin.	12. Front Washer.
5. Chase.	13. Front Pin.
6. Capstan Screw.	14. Front Rail.
7. Key Front.	15. Front Bushing.
8. Balance Rail.	16. Balance Bushing.

UPRIGHT KEYS

This should give the keys a nice smooth finish. Do not sandpaper the key fronts, but carefully use the buffing wheel on these. Some people use a scraper on the keys instead of sandpaper to start with and if you know how to handle a scraper, you may use this if you wish.

For ordinary non-ivory keys, i.e. celluloid keys, one need only use the buffing wheel, using buffing soap sparingly.

If keys are so damaged or worn that they need recovering, it is advisable to send them to the professional key manufacturers for relaying. As ivory is rather expensive nowadays, you may find that keys covered with best grained celluloid will be suitable for your piano, but if you want ivory ask your key manufacturers for prices.

KEY FELTS

These are the front washers, balance washers and backtouch. If these are motheaten remove them, but they must be replaced with exactly the same thickness felt as before. Remove backtouch felt with a sharp chisel. Do not put thicker backtouch felt than the felt removed. If the felt you have is a little thinner than the felt removed, you may make it up with a long strip of suitable felt, e.g. thin boxcloth, nameboard, or some people even use cardboard, $\frac{3}{8}$″ by the length of the keys. The backtouch itself is usually 1″ by the length, or a little more. Glue this strip along the front of the previous position and the thin strip of other material just under the back of the backtouch, but if you are lucky one strip of backtouch, if exactly the same thickness as previously, is all that you will need. Now replace balance washers. These must be exactly the same thickness as washers removed. Next the front washers have to be replaced.

RE-BUSHING KEYS

Chases

If bushing of keys is necessary on the chase, first of all remove the existing red bushing using a sharp pointed knife. Assuming you have purchased the suitable bushing from your Piano Suppliers, measure the width required on your key, cut a length of suitable width and with your knife cut a small point at one end. Insert this bushing point through the slot in the chase at the side. The point should now reach through to the top of the chase. You may need a slim bradawl to push it through the balance pin hole underneath to send the bushing upwards. Pull the bushing through until about $\frac{1}{2}$″ is still showing from the first point of entry. Do this on the other side also with another strip of bushing. Apply a little glue to the top of this bushing, pull through until only $\frac{1}{16}$″ of bushing is still showing through the slot. Make sure that the bushing still has a little glue between itself and the chase (on both strips). Now insert a slim piece of wood into the slot from the top of the chase to hold the glueing of the bushing in place. The Trade has a specially shaped metal plug for this job. When the glueing is set, remove the plug and using your knife,

47

trim and cut away excess bushing. If you have enough plugs you may go through all the work in the same way.

Front Bushings

Remove the bushing to be replaced, keeping a piece for the pattern. Cut similar pieces from the new bushing, apply glue to one side of the bushings and insert the bushings in place, using a special wedge which is required to hold them until the glueing is set.

RECOVERING KEYS

It is possible nowadays to get from the Trade ready shaped plastic key covering, singly to suit key concerned or in sets of $7\frac{1}{4}$ octaves and also a suitable tube of adhesive required for this job.

Of course, if you want to, keys may be recovered by the Trade to give a really professional finish.

REPLACING KEYS ON KEY FRAME

You may find that the keys are tight on the balance pins. If this is so, you must use a special key file. This must not be thicker than the balance pin. Just push the file into the balance pin holes to make it easier to put keys back. Now replace keys on key board. We are now ready to put the action back in the piano.

ADJUSTING PILOTS

Once the action is in place the next thing we must do is to adjust the capstan screws (sometimes called pilot screws), by turning up or down, whichever is required, so that the hammer shank is touching, but not actually resting on the hammer rest felt. These capstan screws have a direct effect through the heel of the lever, through the jack, the notch of the butt, and the hammer shank which is on the hammer rest.

SET OFF

Next we must make sure the set off is correct, by depressing the key or using your finger and lifting the lever just below the check wire, so that the hammer approaches the string. When the nose of the hammer is $\frac{1}{8}''$ from the string, the jack should be drawn away from the notch by the action of the set off button. If the hammer nose blocks, or touches the string, use your set off screwdriver and turn down the set off regulating screw until it is setting off at $\frac{1}{8}''$. If the hammer nose is setting off further away than $\frac{1}{8}''$, turn the regulating screw up to correct set off.

REGULATION TOOLS

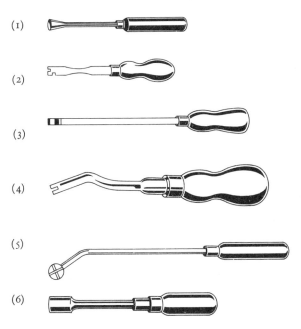

(1)

(2)

(3)

(4)

(5)

(6)

1. Set Off.   4. Key Spacer.
2. Check Bender.   5. Over Damper Crank.
3. Damper Spacer (Crank).   6. Grand Set Off for oblong head screws.

LEVELLING KEYS

Never attempt to level keys without first adjusting the capstan (pilot) screws as mentioned previously. To level keys one must use a key straight edge. The piano trade use a straight edge $3'10'' \times 1\frac{1}{8}'' \times \frac{1}{4}''$ and covered with celluloid. Keys must never be higher than the lock front, i.e. when you look at the top of the lock front at eye level you cannot see under the keys. Lay the straight edge along the keys. If one or two keys are high you will notice that the hammers of the high keys lift off the hammer rest. This can be seen clearly if you gently tap keys with the straight edge, causing the hammers of the high keys to jump off the hammer rest. Remove a high key and using a small bull nose plane, or something similar, plane away a little wood under the key at the balance wire hole. All you need to do is to plane a little wood away trying occasionally to check whether you have removed enough—do not plane the whole length of the key away, but approximately $\frac{1}{2}''$ underneath over the balance wire hole. Once you have levelled the high keys you must deal with those much lower than the rest. You must use paper washers of various thicknesses (usually tissue paper thickness up to thin cardboard thickness). These you may punch out yourself or you can buy these washers ready punched for use in key levelling. If one key is too deep remove it, lifting the balance washer away from the pin, put the paper washer on the pin and then replace the balance washer on top of this. Try with the straight edge that this key is now level with the other keys. Level all keys with this method.

Finally use your eye along the keys and this will tell you if they are all level.

FINAL REGULATION

Finally we are going to go through regulation and for this we use a 2 oz. touch weight. On keys the touch must be $\frac{3}{8}''$ deep. By

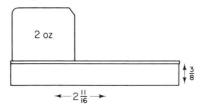

TOUCH WEIGHT

using a touch weight of $\frac{3}{8}''$, when this is placed on the key and depressed, the top of the key at the front must be level with the top of the touch weight which is depressed. Try the touch weight along the keys at odd keys. If they are alright for touch start from the first three notes in the treble, depressing the first key with your middle finger, the next with the index finger and the third with the thumb. These three fingers should be applied as if you were actually playing these notes. When you play these three notes they should set off from the string $\frac{1}{8}''$ (as mentioned before) and drop back into check, i.e. the balance hammer should drop onto the check of the lever. The nose of the hammer should be approximately $\frac{5}{8}''$ from the string. If, for example, the hammer sets off and drops back into check but the nose of the hammer is further than $\frac{5}{8}''$ from the string, hold the bottom of the lever near the check wire and tape wire and with your other hand press the check slightly forward; try note again to make sure that it has dropped into check correctly. Some people use a check bender tool for this. If, on the other hand, the hammers are checked off too close to the string, bend check slightly towards you to correct this. Three notes are played in this case so you can see that the three notes are setting off and dropping back into check together. If you find a note is too deep (use your touch weight), i.e. deeper than $\frac{3}{8}''$, lift up the key, remove front baize and using paper or card washers (these may be obtained from Piano Suppliers, or you may punch them out yourself), place a suitable thickness paper washer, replace on top of this your baize and try note again with touch weight. If touch weight level is correct move to the next note.

When using sharps in this operation, one should not use the touch weight. If when the sharp is pressed down the front of this note goes deeper than the naturals, remove the sharp and baize, put a suitable washer in place and replace the front baize. Try the sharp for touch. When you play the notes—a natural, sharp and a natural together—they should set off and drop into check so that your eye tells you that the hammers are in line with each other and the checks are also in line with each other. Use your fingers between the strings and the noses of the hammers to measure if they are correctly in check. When these three notes are depressed the thickness of an average person's fingers is a suitable guide of the distance from the string to the nose of the hammers of $\frac{5}{8}''$. Continue with the rest of the notes in a similar manner.

DAMPERS AND DAMPER SPOONS

Our next job is to make sure that the dampers lift off the strings at the correct time. The dampers are lifted by the effect of the damper lift spoons, which are fitted on the levers next to the flanges. When the key is depressed, lifting the lever which, in turn, through the jack lifts the hammer towards the string—the correct time for the damper spoon to operate should be when the nose of the hammer reaches exactly above the red nameboard felt on which is glued the white damper felt on the damper. The way to go about this is to start with the first treble damper. Press the key down looking at the hammer nose; if the hammer is only halfway towards the string or thereabouts, and you notice that the damper is just starting to lift from the string, the damper is lifting too soon. With a piece of chalk mark a horizontal line on the wooden part of the hammer, not on the felt. If the next hammer travels completely to the string and still the damper is not lifting, make a vertical mark with your piece of chalk on the wooden part of the hammer, i.e. just above the shank. But, of course, if you

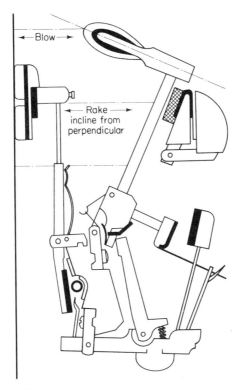

The blow is the distance between the nose of the hammer and the string, which varies in different pianos.

UPRIGHT ACTION BLOW

find that the damper is lifting at the correct time, which is when the nose of the hammer is just above the red felt of the damper, no chalk mark is needed. Go through all the dampers in this manner, marking all the hammers in the correct way.

When all this is done remove the action from the piano. The action should rest on the bench with the dampers away from you. Bend over the action and using the chalk marks as a guide, i.e. if the damper was lifting too soon (horizontal chalk mark will tell you), crank the spoon towards you, with a damper crank making sure to hold the lever with your hand under the check wire and tape wire. It is *important* you hold it in this manner.

If the damper is lifting too late crank the spoon away from yourself, towards the dampers and, of course, do not touch the dampers which are working correctly.

When you have gone through all the dampers in this manner, replace the action in the piano and try the first damper with a chalk mark on it. If it is lifting correctly (after your corrections) use a slightly damp cloth to remove the chalk mark. Try all the dampers in the same way. You may find that you have not cranked enough or you have cranked too much—mark the hammer accordingly. You will find that you have correctly cranked at least half of your dampers. You may have to go through this procedure several times until each damper is working correctly.

OVER DAMPERS—SPRING AND LOOPS

I shall mention briefly repairs on the old spring and loop type action, also with the over dampers. You will have learnt in the previous lessons re-centring, re-facing, recovering notches, cushions, pads and balance hammers. All this knowledge will help you in repairing spring and loop actions, except in the slight differences which I will explain.

You will notice if you are working on a spring and loop action that cushion felt is not used for covering notches and cushions, instead you will be using boxcloth of a suitable thickness. Using the methods of covering as before, cover in boxcloth making sure that the thickness of the boxcloth is the same as that of the old box-cloth which has been removed.

With balance hammers you will notice that leather is not used, but thin check felt. Once again, you must use the same thickness as the original, but unlike the leather on the tape action, which has leather covered on the outside towards the check, the check felt used is on the inside towards the butt.

OVER DAMPER

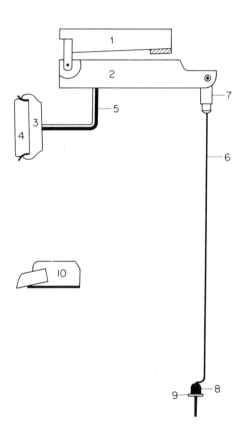

1. Damper Rail.
2. Damper Body.
3. Damper Head.
4. Damper Felt.
5. Damper Wire.

6. Damper Wire.
7. Damper Button fitting.
8. Damper Button.
9. Washer.
10. Treble Damper.

LOOPS

If you have to replace broken loops, you will notice the loop itself comes out near the notch and is plugged and glued with a small piece of wood at the other side of the butt to hold the loop. Using a suitable drill, whilst the butt is held firmly in a vice, carefully drill through the old plug hole, through the butt, until the drill shows itself in the loop hole near the notch. You must use the special loop cord obtainable from the Piano Suppliers. To get this loop cord through the butt easily a piece of thin wire (butt spring wire, gauge 6, will do) about 3″ long is needed. Use this piece of thin wire, bent like a hairpin, with the loop cord threaded through it and push the wire through the butt hole so that the wire shows itself near the notch. Carefully pull through till the loop cord shows. You should now have two ends showing through the butt, where the wire was inserted. Remove the wire from the loop cord. To keep the loop itself in the correct position, it is advisable for you to use an old piece of hammer shank, trimmed with a knife to fit into an already sound loop—being neither too tight nor too loose. Now using this prepared shank, insert it into the newly formed loop. Carefully pull the loop wire tight from the other side and insert a matchstick or similar wood, which has been dipped in glue, into the hole where the loop wire is. Using a sharp knife cut close to the butt, trimming away surplus loop and matchstick. Next remove the prepared shank from the loop itself, i.e. near the notch and you have now completed this operation. You can, of course, use this prepared shank to give you the exact size loop for as many loops as you may wish to replace.

JACKS

On jacks we have a spring, which is attached to the loop of the butt (when in operation) and if this has to be replaced, make sure when ordering the replacement springs from your dealer

SPRING AND LOOP

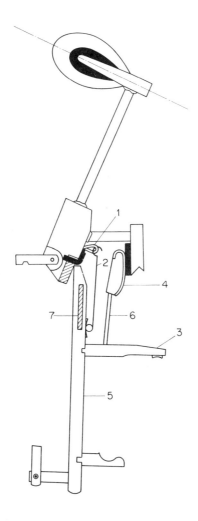

1. Loop.
2. Spring.
3. Bushing Damper wire hole.
4. Check.

5. Jack.
6. Check Wire.
7. Guide Wire felt.

that these are the correct length, as they do vary. The straight length of spring ends in a hook and where the length of spring ends and the hook commences it should be above the jack. Assuming you have removed all the old springs, insert the new spring into the old hole, making sure you have a small felt washer (nameboard is suitable) between the spring and the wood of the jack. This prevents squeaking when being played. Pull the spring wire through until the spring coil and the washer are tight up against the jack. Bend up the wire at the back; use your cutters and cut the excess wire away, so that there is only approximately $\frac{1}{2}''$ of wire showing and with a pair of long-nosed pliers holding the extreme end of the wire, bend this at right angles towards the Jack. Open up your long-nosed pliers so that one side of the pliers is against the top of the spring. Press the pointed bit into the wood, whilst the other side of the pliers is pressing against the wood just above the coil of the spring. With gentle but firm pressure drive the point of the spring into the wood of the Jack, giving it a very firm hold.

LEATHER COVERED JACKS

Remove all leather which is worn with a sharp knife. The jack must be recovered with leather individually, as it is not possible to recover in groups of five. To do this, make a cutting block as mentioned previously. When recovering these jacks individually, making sure you have the correct length and width (see your pattern), and always glue the leather to the top first. When this glueing is set, then glue the rest of the leather.

BUSHING HOLES

If the bushing holes have to be replaced (these bushing holes are, of course, used to guide the damper wire) you may find it difficult to push them out. Use a little methylated spirits, carefully applied to the bushing itself and, usually, the bushing will be easily pushed out. This bushing is usually boxcloth—make sure you have the exact thickness of boxcloth (the same as that removed). You may cut this in a length using a straight edge; approximately 6" length × $\frac{5}{8}$" is used.

Use a knife to cut a small point at one end of your length of boxcloth. Insert this pointed end through the bushing hole from the bottom upwards, pulling it through carefully until only about $\frac{1}{4}$" is showing below the hole. Apply a little glue to this and carefully pull the rest of the bushing through so that a little is still showing below. With your sharp knife cut all the extended length of boxcloth close to the wood. Go through the rest in the same manner.

WORK ON OVER DAMPERS

Over dampers get their name because the dampers are fitted over the hammers. Of course, on modern pianos dampers are fitted below the hammers. If your dampers need re-centring, i.e. if the flanges are tight, unscrew them and re-centre as explained previously. Over dampers are quite different to under dampers and if they have to be recovered, this is the method to use.

First of all it is important to number the dampers, as you are going to unscrew all of them. To ensure you screw them back into the damper wire as before, mark the wire with a fibre-tip pen, close to the wood of the damper, so that when the damper is unscrewed there will be a mark on the wire which you will screw up to when you have completed the recovering.

When you are unscrewing the dampers you may find that the damper wire is rusted into the damper and you must *never* use force to turn out the damper. If your dampers are rusted in, apply a little heat, using your casting lamp, to the damper wire. This will expand the metal and when it is cool it will contract. Carefully try to unscrew the damper and if it still does not move, apply more heat until you are successful. Be careful you do not burn any of the woodwork. Having removed all your dampers, have a saucepan of boiling water and place your damper heads in it. Stir with a stick and you will find all the felt will come away from the wood. When this has happened, tip all of this into a sieve and remove all the wooden damper heads and lay them out to dry, throwing away all old felt. When the damper heads are completely dry, lay out in order from the bass, which is the widest, narrowing down to the treble, all excepting a few treble dampers which are shaped quite differently to the majority. Put these to one side. By looking at the damper head itself you will know which is the top. This will still be slightly discoloured, despite having been boiled and the underneath will usually have a long pencil mark on it. Lay these out on a board in the correct order. These will narrow down gradually making sure that the tops of the dampers are following each other. You now need two strips of wood, $\frac{1}{2}'' \times \frac{1}{2}'' \times$ the length of the damper heads (whatever that might be). Tack the first strip of wood onto your bench—you only need a few tacks to hold this in place—and tack the other strip of wood (same measurements as first strip) to the other side of the dampers, holding the dampers firmly together between the strips. A centre pin knocked into the bench close up against the outside edge of bass and treble (first and last damper) will hold the dampers firmly together on the bench.

Next cut two lengths of red nameboard felt, $\frac{3}{8}'' \times$ the length of the dampers and glue these pieces on the insets. The damper felt which is going to be used is called *end grain* felt. You must purchase this from your Piano Suppliers. This varies in width from $1\frac{1}{4}''$, $1\frac{1}{2}''$, $1\frac{3}{4}''$ to $2''$, so make sure you have the correct width. This will be in a strip. Make sure your glue is hot and using a glue brush, apply glue into the channel, fairly thickly. When this is applied waste no time in inserting the strip of damper felt. Weight and heat are essential to make this glueing good so if you have a long, flat strip of metal heat this carefully (not too hot, just slightly too hot to hold), lay some brown paper on the top along the damper which you have just glued and place the hot length of metal on top of this. Place some weights on top of this metal to press the felt down—two old-fashioned flat irons would do, or something similar.

TREBLE DAMPERS

As you will notice these dampers are quite different. You will need a strip of hammer felt for these dampers, cut to fit in the space in the groove. Assuming, when all your dampers are close together, they measure $5\frac{1}{2}''$ from end to end, use a strip of felt of 6″ and just thick enough to fit into the grooves of the dampers. It is best to keep a piece of the old felt of this type as a pattern. Glue each damper into this strip of felt so that about $\frac{3}{4}''$ is showing from the wood. Glue each damper in the same way, close to the next. When this is done place the dampers in a vice and apply gentle pressure to hold the felt in.

The next day your dampers should be ready for cutting. Remove the strips of holding wood, lift up the dampers, and turn the damper felt down on your cutting board. Now you must get a very sharp knife, not too thick and cut the overlapping felt from the first bass and last treble. Always do this before cutting the remaining dampers. *Very lightly* grease the sides of your knife and carefully cut each damper apart from the next. If you find that some of your glueing has not, in fact, taken, apply glue and press home. Treble dampers must be laid on the bench and, using your pattern, cut away any excess felt at the angle of the pattern. Cut away the first and the last dampers, then cut each damper to separate them.

Having done all this you are now ready to screw back your dampers.

METHOD OF RE-ASSEMBLY

Having done all the necessary work to this action it is now ready for re-assembly. In re-assembling spring and loop actions it is best to fit the jacks first of all. This is done more easily by having the action on your bench upside down, i.e. with the jacks to the top and the jack flanges towards you. Make sure you start from the treble. Screw each one carefully down making sure that the jack is in the correct space between the guide wires. When you have done all this turn the action up the right way and picking up your first treble hammer, loop up to the spring which is on the jack and screw to the action. Complete the rest of this assembly using this method. Screw on hammer rest. Put the action into the piano and square up the hammers to the strings.

REGULATION—SPRING AND LOOP

We need not go over the regulation completely, but only need to deal with the slight differences there are between tape and spring and loop actions. On spring and loop keys there are no pilots or capstans. Instead you will find a screw covered by box-cloth. Once again you must make sure that the hammer shank is just off the hammer rest felt, i.e. it may appear to be resting on it, but there is no weight on the hammer rest felt from the hammer shank. If the hammer is off the hammer rest, remove the key, lift up the boxcloth which is only glued at one end, turn down the screw slightly placing key back in position or, of course, turning up the screw if required. Continue in this fashion until everything is correct. Now level your keys using the method as mentioned before in tape actions.

We are now ready for set off. With this type of action we set off $\frac{1}{16}"$ from the string. Go through the regulation as explained before, but in this case when the hammer is set off $\frac{1}{16}"$, it should drop into check approximately $\frac{1}{8}"$ from the string. If it checks off further away than this use your check bender. Carefully crank the check towards you holding the jack to prevent breakage. When these are all working in the correct manner we are ready to go onto the next stage.

ASSEMBLING DAMPERS

Before actually screwing the damper rail onto the wooden standards make sure the bushing holes, which are on the jacks, into which the damper wire is to be fitted, are open enough to enable the damper wire free movement. If, because of rebushing, the damper wire is too tight one may use a bradawl, which has been heated and insert this into the bushing hole. Once this is done you should find that the damper wire has free movement. Placing the damper rail on top of the wooden standards (this should be done with the action in the piano), do not screw into place yet but insert damper wires into bushing holes. When this is done screw down damper rail to standards. Having recovered your dampers you may find you will have to do a little cranking on the damper wire itself—you will need to use the special crank to do this. One must make sure the damper bodies themselves are all level and are not tight up close to the stop felt on the damper rail. If the damper bodies are close to this, no lifting motion is possible, but if you are lucky you may not have much trouble. However, I have occasionally had to do a lot of work in order to put this right!

We are now going onto the damper wires, which are inserted into the bushing holes of the jack. Go through your regulation from the first treble damper (you have already regulated without the dampers on), making sure that there is a slight movement of the jack before it starts to lift the damper wire. When a note is played the damper should be lifted correctly and when the finger is removed from the key there should be perfect damping. If this is not so make sure that the damper body is not riding on the damper lift rail, which is just below the damper body, or the damper wire riding on the jack on the bushing hole. If it is doing the latter, either screw in the wire deeper or crank up slightly just above the bend of the damper button. But if the former is the case (damper body riding on damper lift rail), it may be caused either by the felt on the standard under the damper lift rail being too thick — if so, replace this — or the loud pedal needs adjusting, allowing the loud stick to be lowered and so prevent the damper rail lifting the dampers too soon.

PEDALS

In many cases, in the older pianos such as the spring and loop, you may find that the pedals are wooden fitted with a brass cap, but all pedals nowadays are metal with brass pedal feet, horn or flat. The flat brass pedal feet are of various sizes: 8″, 9″ and 13″. These usually have a box hinge. The horn pedals, which have a cradle hinge, are usually 9″ in length. The modern small piano has a cradle hinge on the pedal, which is fitted inside the bottom door on the bottom board, but in the older type over damper piano the pedals are fitted underneath and have box hinges. If for any reason you have to replace the pedals of this older type piano, or oil the hinges or tighten up the screws on the hinges, you will have to have the piano lifted up onto its side to get to them (usually firms have a cradle specially made for this purpose). If you decide to change your wooden pedals on your older type piano for brass

PEDAL FEET

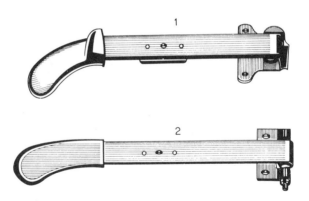

1. Horned with cradle hinge.   2. Flat with flat hinge.

ones, or fit new pedals for any reason, on no account must you try to lift the piano on your own if you are not used to heavy lifting. It usually needs two men to do this job. The way to do this is to bring the piano away from the wall (if near one) and put plenty of cushions or something similar on the floor at the bass end. One person lifts the piano off the floor at the treble end, whilst the other person stands at the side of the piano at the bass end. When the piano is lifted off the floor and the side lowered onto the cushions, this person will prevent the piano dropping heavily onto its side.

Warning: I must emphasise that if you have no experience in lifting, never attempt to lift a piano in any way, as there is a technique in lifting which only comes with experience. It is best to get someone with experience in to do this for you.

Assuming you have the piano on its side, you will find it very easy to change pedals or to do any other necessary work. When this is completed return piano to its original upright position.

For the more modern type of piano, which might need attention, all one has to do is to remove the bottom door. Usually to remove these pedals one has to unscrew the pedal hooks and unscrew the rockers. Also as these pedals will usually have cradle type hinges, you will have to remove the metal screw and nut which passes through the hinge and pedal. By holding the brass pedal foot itself and slightly twisting it, you will find the pedal will come away from the cradle hinge. You may find a large screwdriver helpful. Remove the pedal and unscrew from the cradle hinge the two or three screws holding it to the bottom board. If you are going to replace these pedals with new ones, you must remove the metal screw and nut on the cradle hinge, insert pedal into position, screw down cradle hinge and fit nut and bolt as before.

When you buy new pedals you will find two holes in the metal for the pedal hooks to go into and a piece of leather fitted underneath. Usually this leather has not been drilled in any way. If your pedal hook has to be fitted in the front hole, move the leather so that it is under that hole. Using a suitable size drill push it through the hole onto the leather. This leather should have a little block of wood underneath to make the drilling easier. It will, of course, be removed after drilling. On the other pedal the hole is to the back. Drill accordingly. Fit hooks and rockers and before you screw the nut to the hook, which is through the hole in the rocker, place a piece of front baize washer onto the thread of the hook and then screw on the nut. If not glued, glue the side sticks to the rockers with a piece of felt between the sticks and rockers. In the old spring and loop type piano, there is sometimes a celeste rail instead of a soft pedal. This has two rockers and two side sticks, which are screwed to the insides of the piano in a slot. Before screwing on sticks place a thin baize washer on the screw, then pass the screw through the slot, apply another washer and screw into the hole already there.

PEDAL SPRINGS

The springs on the rockers vary from piano to piano, depending on the make. There are U-shaped pedal springs, spiral pedal springs and flat steel pedal springs.

SPRINGS

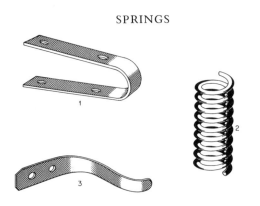

1. U-shape Pedal Spring.   2. Spiral Pedal Spring.
3. Flat Steel Pedal Spring.

CELESTE RAIL

The celeste rail itself must be recovered if it is necessary. The celeste felt can be bought in ready-cut lengths from the Piano Suppliers. You will find the bass end is thicker, so when you replace celeste felt make sure the thicker piece starts at the bass end. Replace celeste rail in the slots provided. Adjust the pedal hook nuts until the celeste rail felt is just below the point on the strings which the hammers will strike. Thus on depressing the pedal the celeste lifts so that when the hammers are struck they strike the celeste felt which softens the notes.

THREE PEDAL PIANOS

Some modern pianos have three pedals. One for the loud pedal, which lifts the dampers from the strings when applied. The middle pedal, when pressed, operates a celeste rail fitted above the hammers. This pedal may also have a slot to the side and when the pedal is pushed into this, the celeste is fixed in position for playing softly and the foot can be removed. The third pedal operates the half-blow, which pushes the hammers forward towards the strings, in fact halving the blow (the distance between the nose of the hammers and the strings). Thus when the piano is played the blow is weaker, making the sound softer.

REPLACING SHANKS

The fitting of a new shank, when required, is a fairly simple thing to do. For example, if the shank is broken in the treble, untape, unscrew and remove the butt from the action—you must, of course, have a suitable shank to replace the broken one (there are various thicknesses, $\frac{1}{2}''$, $\frac{7}{32}''$ and $\frac{1}{4}''$). Cut away the shank close to the head and also close to the butt and using a suitable drill, drill out the old shank which is still in the head and the butt. To do this you may find it easier, when drilling, to have the parts concerned held firmly in a vice. Be very careful when drilling into the head not to drill right the way through. The old shank which is being drilled out, has been set in at exactly the right depth and angle. There should be another $\frac{1}{8}''$ to go before the drill goes right through the head. Of course, if you are lucky enough to have proper machinery and can set this up correctly, you have no problems. It is possible to buy a hammer shank bit with a wooden handle, which tuners usually carry with them in their kit.

When drilling out the butt, drill out approximately $\frac{1}{2}''$ in depth. You may purchase from the trade, if you wish to, a hammer shank extracting tool, which removes shanks from heads or butts without damage, if enough shank is still showing from the break to allow the extracting tool sufficient grip.

Replace butt in action, screw up and tape up. Pick up your new shank and hammer head. You will usually find that to fit the shank into the head it is advisable to 'roll' the shank using two files, one lying on the bench, the shank on top of it and another file pressing onto the shank end which is going to be inserted into the head. With fairly firm pressure roll the shank by moving the file backwards and forwards. This should make an impression of about $\frac{1}{4}''$ on the end of the shank, which is then glued into the head, making sure it is square to the original heads and shanks which are already in place. Now we have to cut the shank to the exact length required.

If you roll the shank, using files as before, on the opposite end, i.e. the end which is going to be inserted into the butt, you can then insert the shank into the butt, but you will find the shank is far too long. Cut away a little of the excess shank and try it once more in the butt. If there is $\frac{1}{16}''$ or so still showing you can file off carefully this excess from the end of the shank. Insert the shank into the butt once more and see that the hammer is correct in every way. Remove shank, apply glue to the end of it, making sure it covers all of the end of the shank and insert into butt. *Note:* It is advisable to use hot glue, as mentioned previously and not tube glue.

If you have drilled out the head correctly, it should be in alignment with the remainder. Also if the butt has been drilled out correctly the top of the balance hammer will be level with those on either side.

Of course, in overstrung pianos, hammers in the bass have the heads at a different angle and this must be taken into account when drilling out.

A FEW OF THE MINOR COMPLAINTS ONE FINDS IN A PIANO

Clicking Noises

1. This can be caused by missing cushion felt, thus causing the jacks to make slapping noises against the wood where cushion felt should be glued.
   Remedy—Untape, unscrew the hammer flange, glue a suitable thickness of cushion felt in place, re-screw and re-tape in the piano.
2. Clicking noise caused by the hammer head loose in the shank, or a balance hammer loose in the shank.
   Remedy—Remove the head completely and re-glue or remove the balance hammer completely and re-glue.
3. Tape wire touching the side of the next check wire when played.
   Remedy—Bend slightly away from the next check wire.

Sticking Note

1. If the key, when pressed down, sticks—remove the key and use easing pliers to ease, replace the key in position.
2. Key or keys catching on the lock front of an Upright piano. If the lock front of the piano cannot be removed by unscrewing

69

from underneath, but is glued permanently into position, re-move the keys from the position where they are sticking when depressed and, to make the space between the key and the lock front greater, drive a suitable piece of wood between the front rail and the lock front, thus forcing the lock front slightly away from the key itself. This piece of wood should not be higher than the front rail itself once in place.

If the lock front can be removed by screws underneath, unscrew and remove and glue a thin strip of cardboard or veneer to the back of the lock front and re-screw into position. This will have the effect of causing the lock front to come away slightly from the keys when they are in place.

If the same trouble applies this identical method can be used in a Grand key front which is the same as a lock front on an Upright (that is, it is situated in front of the keys).

No repetition on Upright Pianos

The jack centres maybe tight or the spiral spring weak or the spiral spring not in the correct position under the jack.

Remedy—Re-centre the jack; strengthen the spring or replace it; position the spiral spring correctly under the jack.

These are but a few of the many problems one may find in pianos, but if you actually carry out all the work mentioned in this book on repairs, plus using common sense, you should be able to deal with any problems that may arise.

GRAND PIANOS

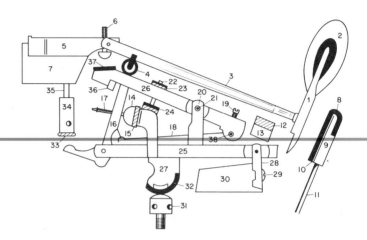

1. Hammer Head.	21. Centre Pin.
2. Hammer Felt.	22. Regulating Screw.
3. Hammer Shank.	23. Regulating Felt Washer.
4. Hammer Shank Roller.	24. Regulating Felt Washer.
5. Hammer Shank Flange.	25. Lever Body.
6. Grand Set Off Screw.	26. Lever Carriage.
7. Hammer Rail.	27. Lever Heel.
8. Check Leather.	28. Lever Flange.
9. Check.	29. Flange Screw.
10. Check Underfelt.	30. Lever Rail.
11. Check Wire.	31. Capstan Screw.
12. Hammer Rest Felt.	32. Lever Heel Boxcloth.
13. Hammer Rest Rail.	33. Escapement Felt.
14. Jack Regulating Button.	34. Escapement Dolly.
15. Jack Regulating Felt.	35. Escapement Dolly Wire.
16. Lever Jack.	36. Jack Pad.
17. Jack Regulating Screw.	37. Stop Pad.
18. Lever Spring.	38. Bushing and Pin holding spring in place.
19. Grub Screw.	
20. Bushing Cloth.	

GRAND PIANOS

THE REMOVAL OF FALL, KEY SLIP AND KEY BLOCKS

We will assume that everything has to be done to a roller type action, so first of all we remove the following items:

First the fall—this is done by holding the fall at the front and just lifting it towards you. But in a very well known piano you have to remove the key slip (key front), unscrew the key blocks, then, when lifting the fall out, the key blocks which are fitted to the fall itself, will just come off the pivot pins which are holding them. Also, you will find a spring fitted on the bass key block. In other pianos remove the key slip (key front) which is screwed in underneath the front, or just pressed into place on dowels. Next remove the key blocks by unscrewing the wing nuts or screws which are underneath the front of the piano, below the key blocks.

THE REMOVAL OF ACTION AND KEYS

To remove action and keys place your hands each end of the key front rail, at the sides where the key block pins are located. Care must be taken not to push down any of the keys with your fingers or by your body pressing onto them in case a shank is broken as you pull the action and keys out of the piano towards you. Pull the keys and action right out of the piano and put them on your bench. Next we must remove the action from the keys. To do this we must unscrew the screws on the action standards. There may be four or five, depending on the type of piano you have. These are screwed onto the key bed itself with screws at the

73

front and back. Once these are removed you merely lift the action up and away from the keys, if it has capstan screws fitted on the keys. But sometimes, in a certain German piano, they have small prolonges fitted to the keys themselves, which are fitted in a slot and held by a pin. If your piano is of this type you must, by pressure on the key itself with one hand near to the prolonges, insert your other hand under the lever, lift up and the prolonge will be pulled out of its seating. Do this to all the prolonges before attempting to remove the complete action away from the keys. Once removed put the keys aside for the moment.

GRAND ACTION REPAIR

First of all we will remove the hammers and by using the term hammers, as in the case of the upright piano, we mean the hammers themselves, the shanks and the flanges. Before we unscrew the same it is always best to take a 'scale'. To do this we need a long thin strip of wood, to reach the whole length of the action, $1''$ wide by its length, thickness immaterial but I suggest nothing thicker than $\frac{1}{4}''$. If you have this 'scale' stick lay this along the shanks, close up to the hammers and push it towards the bass end where you will have a block of wood (you may wish to use your sandpapering block) close up against the first bass standard. Slide the scale stick close to this block and remove the block. Using a pencil carefully mark on the scale stick the exact centre of the shank of the first bass hammer. Do the same to the next and so on through the remainder up to the last treble hammer. This will help you when you are re-assembling the hammers and must be used to show you exactly where they were originally.

Remove the scale stick and unscrew the hammers by the screws on the flanges. Place these screws in a suitable tin and mark it 'hammers'. This is important because these screws are usually much longer than the lever screws. Your hammers must now be in order on a suitable tray. Put these aside until needed.

REMOVE LEVERS

To remove levers all you do is to stand the action on its front, on the bench, so that the screws and flanges of the levers are at the top, making it easier for you to uncsrew them. Start this from the first treble one working right through to the last bass lever, placing the levers, as you remove them, on a suitable tray and the screws in a box.

All that remains of the action now are the hammer rail, lever rail, hammer rest and standards. Leave all these assembled as they are, but if they are in a dirty condition it is advisable to clean them at this point ready for the re-assembling of the levers and hammers when they have been repaired.

GRAND LEVER REPAIRS

We will assume that all the centre pins are tight for the flanges, jacks and carriages. Using the method of removing centre pins as mentioned before in re-centring Upright pianos, have a suitable tray on which to place the various parts, making sure to keep them in the correct order. First remove the flange, next the jack and lastly the centre pin of the carriage. When you have removed the carriage centre pin you will find that to remove this from the lever body itself, you will have to remove the rocker regulating screw, which will have two pads, one above and one below the carriage. Although this is a screw and can be turned with a screwdriver, you may find that using a pair of pliers to carefully grip the head of the screw and turning the lever body itself will be an easier method of unscrewing.

Warning: One point I must mention is that in some cases the rocker regulating screw may have rusted into the lever body itself, so unscrew very carefully indeed to avoid the screw breaking off, leaving part of it in the lever body, which would cause you a lot of trouble. However, through my own experience I have found that only 1 in 1,000 Grand actions has this problem of rusting in these particular screws.

Once all these screws are removed put together with them the pads which are related to each screw, i.e. the top rocker regulating pad and the underneath one. Put these in a container for safe keeping.

It is very rarely that Grand actions have to have their springs replaced, but if they have to be replaced you will need to have three patterns to take to the Piano Suppliers, i.e. an extreme treble one which is the thinnest of the springs, a middle spring, which is the next gauge up and a bass one which is the thickest of the three. These springs are usually held in place by bushing and a piece of wire through the bushing. When re-fitting the new springs pull the bushing through first to hold the spring cut in close to the carriage, then fit a very thin centre pin (a 20 will do) and cut close again. If you are pulling the bushing through, *do not glue* bushing for springs as in flanges. It is possible, if you wish, to use a matchstick to push in the hole to hold the spring.

Care must be taken to mark which is the bass and which is the treble on the carriages and when you fit the new springs you must be careful to have the treble in the treble end, the middle and the bass in the correct places. If you have the treble up the bass end you will find that the treble spring in the bass will be far too weak to operate correctly and if the bass is up the treble end they will be far too strong. This is all to do with the weight of the hammers being different in bass and treble and the springs are made to operate to carry the relative weights of the hammers, light in treble gradually getting heavier towards the bass.

RECOVERING JACK PADS AND ROCKER STOP PADS

If the jack pads have to be replaced it is essential that the felt used is exactly the same thickness as the felt removed. You may use cushion felt or parallel damper felt of the correct thickness.

Cut off in strips exactly as your patterns and into individual pieces to fit into the space on the carriage. It is a good idea to make and use a cutting block, as mentioned in Upright repairs. Make sure, when you are glueing these pieces of felt, not to let any glue get onto the front of the pad where the jack is actually going to press. With regards to the rocker stop pads, these are usually leather and must be replaced by the same. After removing the old leather replace and glue as the originals.

RE-CENTRING LEVERS

As the method of re-centring has been described under Upright repairs, there is no need to mention it again here. The first things to re-centre are the flanges. Next the carriages. There is no need to screw the rocker regulating screw in when this is done but re-centre the jacks next. It is essential, when re-centring, that there is no tightness in the centre pin bushing whatsoever, but also no side play, and the centre pin should be held firmly in the wood of the centre pin hole. This has been mentioned before in re-centring, but its importance cannot be overstressed. The lever spring must now be hooked up onto the loop, which is on the jack. Some people apply a tiny bit of grease onto the hook of the spring where the loop is under pressure at this point. This prevents squeaking.

The next thing to do is to replace the rocker regulating screw, making sure that the rocker regulating pads are sound and have no moth-eaten parts. If these need replacing do so. Screw in position as before, with the top rocker regulating pad in place and the underneath one fitted below the carriage. It is a very good idea, before screwing into the wood of the lever body, to put a little Japanese wax on the screw itself, which will enable the screw to move easily for adjustment. Turn the screw down so that the carriage itself is level with, or just slightly above the level of the jack. At this point, whilst doing this, one may also adjust, if necessary, the jack regulating screw, making sure the jack is in

77

alignment with the mark on the carriage top. This is to ensure that when the action is assembled the jack is correctly placed under the roller. Whilst doing all the work to the lever, it is a good idea to check that the lever heel boxcloth is sound. If this is not then replace it with exactly the same thickness as before. When all this has been done, screw the levers back onto the lever rail.

REPAIRING HAMMERS

Re-centre hammer flanges, using method as described previously. I will now describe a method of recovering rollers. We will assume that both the leather and white boxcloth (underneath the leather) on the roller need recovering. It is possible, by the way, for you to buy complete sets of rollers for replacement. This includes the piece of wood on which they are glued, but for the purpose of the book, here is the method for recovering the leather and boxcloth. With a very sharp knife carefully cut through the leather and boxcloth so that the knife touches the roller wood itself. Usually, you also find that where the roller is inserted into the hammer shank, there is a little glue on the hammer shank and the leather. Placing the knife on the hammer shank, carefully cut into and up to the wood of the roller on both sides. This will leave the leather and boxcloth underfelt cut open and exposed to the wood of the roller. Carefully cut away with the knife, taking care not to damage the wood itself. This can be a very difficult job, so take extra care with your knife, as it is easy to cut oneself.

Assuming all the leather and boxcloth underfelt has been removed from the complete set, the white boxcloth is replaced first of all. This must be of exactly the same thickness as the boxcloth removed. Cut enough of this strip of boxcloth to completely cover the roller wood itself, from one side of the hammer shank around to the other side of the hammer shank. Cut these pieces the width of the roller wood, enough to cover the complete set.

GLUEING AND TRIMMING
ROLLER UNDERFELT

To do this you will need a glue stick and a spring of the hammer covering type. Apply glue to the wood of the roller, which is still fitted into the hammer shank and wrap the white boxcloth around this. Apply the spring which will hold this in place. Go through the whole set in this way. If you are only using ten of these springs for your glueing, when the tenth roller underfelt is glued into place, it is possible to remove the first spring from the roller, which can then be used to hold the eleventh glueing. Next remove the second spring, which can be used for the twelfth glueing and so on throughout the set.

RECOVER ROLLERS

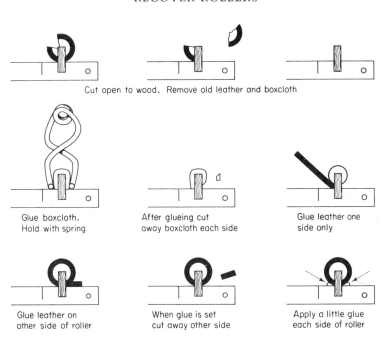

Cut open to wood. Remove old leather and boxcloth

Glue boxcloth.
Hold with spring

After glueing cut
away boxcloth each side

Glue leather one
side only

Glue leather on
other side of roller

When glue is set
cut away other side

Apply a little glue
each side of roller

79

When all this glueing is finished and the glueing has set hard, use your sharp knife to trim away a little of the underfelt from the actual shank and just over $\frac{1}{16}''$ up on the felt itself, removing a long strip of felt with your knife. This will leave a piece of the wood of the roller exposed. This must be done on both sides of the roller.

RECOVER LEATHER

You may buy leather in strips ready for recovering rollers. This is usually just over 1″ by whatever the strip or length might be. Next, with the strip of leather you cut individual pieces, $\frac{7}{16}'' \times 1\frac{1}{4}''$ (the strip), with your cutting block. When all these pieces have been cut for your set, 85 or 88, depending on whether you are repairing a 7 or 7¼ Octave Piano (85 or 88 note), apply glue along the wood of the roller which you have previously exposed. From now on we are going to call the white boxcloth the under-roller. The glue should also be applied to the lower part of the under-roller, but not over the top of it.

Once this is done no time must be wasted in inserting the piece of leather in place, because if the glueing gets a chill on it it will not glue properly. Use your knife to press the leather firmly into position. A little touch of glue should now be applied—you may use a pointed matchstick for this purpose—along the leather and the shank. Do this to all the rollers in the set. When the glue is set hard you next apply glue along the other side of the roller on the exposed wood and a little on the under-roller itself, not too far up towards the top of the roller. With your finger apply pressure to the leather on the side which is already glued, rolling the leather close to the other side to which you have just applied glue. Still holding this in position with your finger, carefully force the leather with your knife into the space which is glued. This will appear to be a completed roller, except for the extra piece of leather which is pointing out from the glueing. Leave this exactly in place, as this will hold the leather in position until the glue is set hard. Do this to all the rest of the rollers. Make sure there is no gap between the under-roller and the leather but that it is smooth and tight fitting. When all this is done and the glueing is set hard, use a very sharp knife to cut away carefully the excess piece of leather from the roller. Once again using a pointed matchstick, apply a thin strip of glue along the shank and roller where the excess leather has been removed. This will give additional strength to the roller. If you have been successful you should now have a complete roller. Use this technique on all the remaining rollers. In many cases only the leather needs to be recovered, so just remove the leather alone, leaving the underfelt intact. Cut and glue leather as mentioned above.

RE-ASSEMBLING HAMMERS

The next thing to be done is to re-assemble hammers to the hammer rail. This completed, now, using your scale stick, lay this along the shanks close onto the hammers and, placing a block of wood close to the action standard in the bass end, slide the bass of the scale stick close up against it, then remove block. The scale stick should now be lying exactly as it was when you took the scale and you will find that most of the hammers need adjustment to the markings you made previously on the scale. Slightly un-screw the flange screw and carefully move the shank so that it is in alignment with the mark on the scale stick. Go through all the hammers in the same way, making sure all the spacing is correct.

RE-FACING HAMMERS

We can re-face Grand hammers in a similar way to that explained in Uprights, but another method is as follows:

Lift all the hammers up off the hammer rest itself, so that they are almost vertical, standing on their own on the flanges. Now lay a piece of paper (long enough to cover all the levers throughout the set) along the levers and hammer rest rail. This is to prevent dust getting into the levers. Drop the hammers back down as before, but this time they will be over the paper you have laid along the levers. Lay your scale stick across the shanks just above the hammer rest rail and using string, tie this rail onto the various standards along the set or onto the hammer rail itself. This should hold the hammers firmly in place. If the paper prevents you from tying the string where you want to, just make a hole in the paper for this purpose. We will now use medium glass paper. From a sheet of glass paper cut a strip 1½″ by the length of the sheet. Start to sandpaper the hammers carefully. Have the hammers facing nearest to you, i.e. with the hammer rail away from you and holding one end of the sandpaper, lay it, held in your fingers, close to the nose and with your other hand apply two or three fingers to the smooth side of the sandpaper—the rough side being pressed onto the hammer felt. The hand which is holding the sandpaper must now draw the sandpaper towards you. At the same time press on the sandpaper with the fingers of your other hand. This will gently sandpaper the hammer felt itself from just

RE-FACING HAMMERS

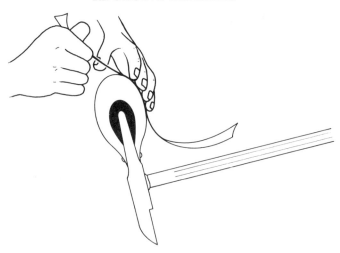

The hand holding the sandpaper draws the sandpaper up towards you. The fingers of your other hand apply gentle pressure on the sandpaper on the Hammers.

below the rivet up to the nose. Go carefully through all the hammers in the same way. Be especially careful in the treble area not to sandpaper through to the wood.

The idea of re-facing is to give the hammers a new lease of life and a pear-shaped appearance. Having done one side of the hammer, turn the action completely around, with the hammer rail towards you. Apply exactly the same method to the other side of the hammers. When this is completed, brush away all the dust and apply white chalk over the hammers themselves.

Note: You will find that generally, in this operation, you will have to use many strips of medium sandpaper.

Now using fine sandpaper go through all the operations once more. This will give the finishing touch to your hammers. Using a small brush (of the scrubbing brush type), brush over all the hammers removing excess chalk dust. When using the brush, brush upwards only from the shank to the nose and do the same to the other side of the hammer—*not* crossways from bass to treble, as the hammers, still being spaced apart, may get damaged. Remove string and scale stick. Finally, we must remove the dust from the sides of the hammers, so lift the first treble hammer with one hand, just slightly higher than the hammers lying on the hammer rest rail and brush the side of the hammer upwards, about three times. Do this to both sides of the hammer. Drop this back to the hammer rest rail and repeat this operation on the next hammer, working your way right through the set. If this is not done, when the action is back in the piano and is being played, you usually get a miniature dust storm! Blow away all dust from the paper which is covering the levers and lift up the hammers to remove the paper.

SPACING LEVERS

This is to be the final operation in your grand action repair. The levers must be spaced correctly to prevent the lever lifting or touching the adjoining roller. This would cause the next hammer to rise simultaneously with the hammer which should be operating when played. To do this have the hammer rail away from you, lift up all the hammers and the lever screws which are in front of you. Starting from the first treble lever make sure that it is in alignment with the hammer shank and roller. If this needs squaring up just release the flange screw slightly, moving the lever so that it is in line with the shank concerned. Tighten up. Use this method going right through the set. If you find that when you tighten up the lever, for example, is still too far to the right of the position it should be in, you must cut a strip of thin paper, $\frac{1}{16}$" × the length of the flange, unscrew the lever flange a little, place your piece of long thin paper between the flange and the lever rail, on the left-hand side and tighten up the screw. This should have the effect of bringing the lever to the left. If one piece of paper is not enough, apply another on top, until you are satisfied with the lever's position. Of course, if any of the other levers, after tightening up, are going to the left, then apply the paper to the right-hand side between the flange and the lever rail. When you are satisfied that all the levers are correctly spaced, drop all the hammers back onto the hammer rest rail and look along it. You should see that the rollers are riding on the carriages correctly.

HAMMER REST RAIL

If you have had to recover the hammer rest rail, use exactly the same thickness hammer rest felt as the original. If you remove the hammer rest rail from its position, make sure that it is exactly in the same position as before when you tighten up the bolts. In some pianos, the hammer rest rail is held by long bolts along the rail with a nut below the hammer rest rail on which it is seated, and another nut screwed into the top to hold this down. If the lower nut is turned too far down or too high this will be in an incorrect position.

GRAND DAMPERS

To repair dampers we must first of all remove the dampers them-selves from the strings of the piano. This means the damper heads themselves which are attached to the damper wires. These damper wires pass through the bushing of the guide rail and are fitted to the damper block, in which they are inserted and held in position by a screw.

However, before removing them look at the damper lifting

GRAND DAMPERS

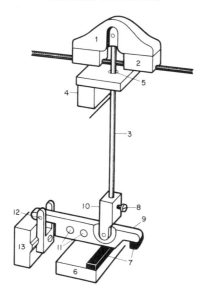

1. Damper Head.
2. Damper Felt.
3. Damper Wire.
4. Damper Guide Rail.
5. Damper Bushing Wire Hole.
6. Damper Lifting Rail.
7. Felt.

8. Damper Block Screws.
9. Damper Body.
10. Damper Block.
11. Leads.
12. Centre Pin and Bushing.
13. Damper Lever Rail.

rail, which is situated underneath the damper bodies themselves. As the term suggests, the damper lifting rail is used to lift the dampers when pressure is applied to the loud pedal on the lyre. Place your fingers under the damper lifting rail and lift it up until the damper lifting rail felt is in contact with the damper bodies themselves, but not actually lifting the dampers off the strings. Place a small block of wood on the key bed, under the damper lifting rail, exactly the thickness required to hold this rail in the position described. If you do not have a small block of wood thick enough for this, it is possible to use a slightly thinner piece of wood into which is inserted a screw. This screw can be adjusted to the height required to hold the damper lifting rail, which is in close contact through the felt to the bodies. The idea of this is that, when all the dampers have been removed and all the work is completed on them and they are being placed back in position, by inserting once again the block of wood (as above) under the damper lifting rail, you will be absolutely sure that the dampers are going to be in exactly the same position as they were before being removed. So when you tighten up the screw which holds the damper wires, you will have less trouble in finishing the job.

REMOVING THE DAMPERS

After completing the above, use a pair of pliers to grip the damper block screw carefully, slightly unscrew and, holding the damper head itself with the other hand, lift the damper out. Place this on a tray and proceed until all dampers are removed. You will notice that this screw can be turned by a screwdriver, but in my experience pliers are better, because a screwdriver tends to cause the damper wire to bend when pressure is applied, whereas with pliers you do not have to exert any pressure forwards, merely grip tightly and turn. Do not unscrew these screws too far as they may get lost. Unscrew just enough to release the pressure on the damper wire.

REMOVE DAMPER STOP RAIL

The damper stop rail is situated just above the damper bodies and is usually held firmly in position by four or five screws in slots, which are there so that adjustment up or down can be carried out as required, that is when the dampers are being re-assembled. Unscrew and remove the damper stop rail.

REMOVING DAMPER BODIES

To remove the damper bodies onto which are attached the damper block and flanges, which are screwed to the damper lever rail which, in turn, has the damper lifting rail attached to it, we must remove the damper lever rail by unscrewing the screws holding it in position. There are slight differences in each piano, i.e. there may be only two screws, one each end of the rail or four, one each end and the other two spaced evenly along the rail. Remove these screws and you can then pull out the damper lever rail with all its attachments. Next, we remove the damper lifting rail by unscrewing the flanges, which are on the damper lifting rail arm. Some pianos have instead of this method a block at each end with a pin through it. But as we cannot go through all the pianos with their various methods of fixing damper lifting rails, we shall only describe the aforesaid type of damper lifting rail arm and flange. Having removed this, we now go onto the flanges. Once again, we shall assume that they all need re-centring, so unscrew all the flanges and as the method of recentring has already been covered, re-centre flanges and damper blocks. Once this is done, screw back into position on the damper lever rail. Also, re-centre the flanges on the damper lifting rail arms. Recover felt on the damper lifting rail, making sure the felt is exactly the same thickness as the felt removed. Screw all this back into the piano as fitted originally.

DAMPER GUIDE RAIL

Unscrew the damper guide rail from the position in which it is fitted, just below the strings and take this out of the piano. This may be in two or three lengths. Check that the bushing is sound. If this needs replacing, remove by applying a little methylated spirits to the bushing itself and you will find it easy to push out. Once this is done, keep this piece of bushing as a pattern for thickness and width. Once you have the bushing of exactly the same type as the original, cut a length of this, making sure the width is the same as the pattern. With a knife cut a point at one end of this length. Insert the point through the bushing hole from underneath upwards and pull through the length of bushing until about $\frac{1}{2}''$ is left below. Apply a little glue to the bushing at this point and pull the rest through, leaving a little bushing still visible below. Using a razor blade or very sharp knife, cut away the length at the top of the damper guide rail absolutely flush. It is really best to do this when the glue is hardened, but this is not essential—it just prevents the knife becoming smeared with glue. If they all need re-bushing, use this procedure throughout. Once this is done, try a damper wire in the hole and if it is slightly tight you must use a bradawl, which has been heated until slightly too hot to touch. Insert this into the bushing hole (this bradawl must be only slightly thicker than the damper wire), remove, try the damper wire again and, if it moves freely, go through all the bushings and try the same. Once this has been done, screw the damper guide rail back into position, below the strings.

Now screw the damper stop rail back in position. You will usually find that the screws which also have washers, have made an impression on the rail itself, so it is best to screw it back in exactly the same position as before removal. If it has no impression where the screw and washer were tightened up before, just slide the stop rail to the top of the slots and tighten up to hold. We will deal with the exact position of the damper stop rail before we have finished with the dampers.

RECOVERING DAMPERS

Grand dampers are larger than Upright dampers so make sure when ordering that you get the correct size. If you are to recover all the dampers the same method is used in recovering as explained in recovering Upright dampers, but we will go over it briefly once again. The single bass dampers consist of clip dampers, the bi-chords have wedge dampers and over the break, where the steel strings usually begin, we have a few split wedge. However each piano is slightly different over the break—some Grand pianos have a few split wedge followed by a few more parallel damper felts to the front and split wedge to the back. Then they carry on through to the treble just with parallel. So you must make a point of noting the exact damper felt required for your particular piano, as you will have to recover them in exactly the same way. It is advisable, before you strip dampers, to make a written record to avoid mistakes. The clip and wedge dampers for recovering are obvious because you can look at the strings themselves, but in the case of split wedge dampers over the break, especially if they have split wedge going on to split wedge with parallel, it is best to have a written record of the numbers and types required.

Strip off all the dampers and recover as mentioned in Upright dampers. The best thing to do, however, is to buy from the manufacturers dampers already cut and backed with red felt, making sure, of course, that the parallel is exactly the same thickness as the dampers removed. Glue damper felts in position.

RE-FIT DAMPERS

Now that the damper lever rail and damper lifting rail are once more in position, place the block of wood which was placed in position to use as a guide before removing the dampers, underneath the lifting rail.

TRIAL DAMPERS

We shall now place a few dampers in position to ensure that when all the dampers are fitted they will be in the correct position. Pick out from the treble dampers the fifth one along, insert this in the bushing of the guide rail through into the damper block. Line up this damper exactly to the strings with one hand and with a pair of pliers in the other hand, tighten up the damper block screw to hold in position. Now from the break end towards the treble take the fifth damper from this position and fit as the previous one. Over the break towards the bass fit the fifth wedge damper. Finally in this exercise we place the fifth damper from the first bass, single clip, in position. (It is advisable to have the damper lyre bolted in position when fixing the dampers.) Having fitted these four dampers in position, now remove the guide block from under the damper lifting rail. Try the loud pedal to see that the dampers are all lifting simultaneously. Push the damper blocks slightly backwards so that when the damper, action and keys are pushed into position they do not catch on them in any way. Place the action and keys on the keyboard. Press down the loud pedal on the lyre —this will lift all the damper bodies up—now push home the keys and action into position. If you do not push the loud pedal while all the dampers are off, you will find it impossible to insert the action and keys completely.

Now we must try the key which will lift the fifth damper from the treble. When the key is being depressed the hammer will begin to rise from its position towards the string. When it has reached two-thirds of its way towards the string the damper should then start to lift. If this is lifting correctly try the other three dampers in the same way.

Extreme problems may be found when not using a guide block but the following methods may also be used for slight adjustments:

Dampers Lifting too soon

If, for example, you find that the damper is lifting immediately the hammer is starting to rise, this must be corrected. Remove the action and the keys from the piano, unscrew the damper block screw slightly, move the damper block slightly higher up the wire and tighten the screw on the block. Do this to the other three dampers if they are also lifting too soon. Slide action and keys into position, using the same method as before. Depress the key and see that the hammer starts to lift the damper when it has travelled two-thirds of the way towards the string.

Dampers Lifting too late

If you find that dampers are lifting too late, i.e. the hammer travels virtually to the string before the damper starts to lift, or even does not lift at all, here is the procedure. Remove action and keys from the piano and using pliers slightly unscrew the damper block screw; lower the damper block down slightly and then tighten the screw. Do this to the other three dampers if they need the same adjustment. Insert action and keys into piano using the method mentioned previously. Try the hammer once more and if, when the hammer has travelled two-thirds of the way towards the string the damper starts to ride, this is once more correct.

Note: *The distance between the nose of the hammer and the string is called the 'blow'.*

The dampers which are lifting too soon or too late should not be too extreme in your piano if the damper felts are exactly the same thickness as the damper felts which were replaced and also if you used the damper block as described above.

Assuming that the four trial dampers are lifting correctly fit all the remaining dampers in position, making sure that the dampers are in alignment with the strings. Then remove the guide block. One thing you *must* do is to put a slight chalk mark on top of the four trial dampers you have been using, which are lifting correctly.

and they should be used as guides to the others. Place your foot on the loud pedal and by giving slight lifting movements look along the dampers. If any dampers are lifting before the marked guide dampers, adjust so they do lift at exactly the same time as the four guide dampers. If the dampers are lifting later than the guide dampers adjust accordingly. This can be a rather long and tedious job but it is essential that they should lift correctly.

MAKING SURE THE DAMPERS DAMP

All the dampers are now lifting together correctly, so we must now make sure the dampers actually damp. Press down the loud pedal, run your finger along the strings from the break to the treble; release foot from pedal and the dampers should now damp correctly. If you find that a parallel damper does not damp correctly it could be that it is not in true alignment with the string— if so adjust accordingly. Sometimes the front part of the damper is on the string whilst the back part of the felt is slightly off the string. If this is the case lift the damper off the string and holding the damper head itself, bend down carefully to adjust. Usually, however, the parallel dampers give you the least trouble. With the split wedge dampers the damper must drop correctly into position —make sure the damper is actually touching the three strings which make the one note. Also in the wedge dampers make sure the two strings making the one note are damping correctly. Only perseverance and common sense will tell you when the dampers are satisfactory but the aforesaid methods of adjustment should help you in any problems you may have. But, in many cases, you will find no trouble whatsoever if you followed the instructions above.

SETTING THE DAMPER STOP RAIL

The damper stop rail which is situated behind the damper wires just above the damper bodies, which you have previously screwed in position, can now be set correctly. (I must mention here that by the adjustment on the damper lift rod the damper lifting rail should be just below the damper bodies but not actually touching them.) Depress loud pedal—this makes dampers and damper bodies lift to their highest. Whilst in this position unscrew the damper stop rail screws slightly and lower the rail until the rail felt nearly touches the damper bodies and tighten up the screws when in this position. You should find when the action and keys are in the piano that when a key is depressed, the damper is off the strings and if you actually hold the damper in your fingers, there should be a very slight lift before it touches the damper stop rail. This damper stop rail, if set in the correct position, will prevent dampers jumping higher than they should when being played. If they in fact do jump higher than they should, they give a slight jolt to the fingers.

REGULATION OF ACTION AND KEYS

In Grand pianos, unlike Upright pianos, levelling of keys is done without the action being fitted to the keys. We will remove the keys from the key frame. We must now examine the backtouch felt, balance washers and front washers. If these need replacing remove them, but make sure the backtouch is replaced by *exactly* the same thickness backtouch felt and the same goes for the balance and front washers. Also check up on the felt at the back of the key which lifts the dampers. Once again, great care must be taken to ensure that the same thickness felt is used.

We have explained previously on Upright keys how to do the bushing on chases and the bushing for the front pin, so we do not need to describe this again. If all felts are now replaced or are in good condition we are now ready to put the keys back on the key frame, but before we do this it is advisable to obtain a special key file. This is a round file which must be exactly the size of the balance pin and use no other thickness. It is always advisable to insert this round file into the balance pin before replacing keys on frame, but if you cannot obtain a key file and the keys slip onto the balance

93

pin easily, you need not worry. Once all the keys are replaced on the key frame try each key individually for free movement. If at all tight in the chases or the bushing to the front pin, these keys must be eased with special key easing pliers. Insert one side of the pliers into the bushing and apply the other to the side of the key. Widen the gap slightly by careful pressure on the pliers. Be careful not to overdo the pressure. If the front bushing of the key has too much side-play (the front pin itself is flat), use your key spacer and slightly turn the pin to the left or the right. Many people in the Trade call this a cricket bat pin as the bit inserted into the front rail is round like a cricket bat handle and the rest protruding is like the cricket bat blade. Make sure all the keys have free movement.

LEVELLING OF GRAND KEYS

Levelling Grand keys is a difficult if not an impossible task with the action fitted to the keys, so we must use some special weights for this purpose. Some people use the round lead weights which are used in key weighting (one weight on top of the other with a long pin through them protruding a $\frac{1}{4}''$ beyond the leads, to hold the leads together, weight approximately 3 ozs.) or one may buy special weights for this purpose. Remove the first key from the frame and, placing your weight as near to the damper check wire as possible, gently tap this with the pin through it to hold it in position. Do this to each and every key in turn.

LEVELLING GRAND KEYS

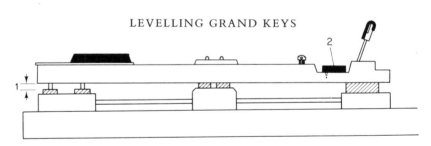

1. Touch $\frac{3}{8}''$.   2. Special 3oz. weight used to help levelling Grand Key.

Next we use a key straight edge. Place the key straight edge along the front of the naturals (white keys) and by a gentle tapping movement you will know which keys are slightly too high. Lift these off the balance pin and plane a little off the underneath of the key at the balance pin hole. Replace in position, apply the key straight edge once more and if there are any lower than the rest, lift these up off the balance pin and place a suitable paper washer underneath the felt washer. It is possible to buy from the Manufacturers balance rail paper washers of various thicknesses which are used in key levelling, also paper and card touch washers for the front rail. Once you have levelled all the front keys correctly go over the sharps in the same way. Now remove all weights from the back of the keys.

FITTING ACTION TO KEYS

Place the action in position on the keys and screw down the action standards in position. The first thing we do now is to level the hammers just slightly off the hammer rest felt. This is done by adjustment of the capstan screw which is on the key itself, on which the lever heel and felt are resting. Obviously, if the hammer is too high off the hammer rest one turns down the capstan. Once this is done and all the hammers are level and slightly off the hammer rest, run your finger across the keys near to the action. If, in fact, the hammers are just off the hammer rest correctly, they will ripple slightly. If you find one or two hammers do not move, turn up the capstan very slightly. Once this is all done satisfactorily, slide the action and the keys into position in the piano.

PREPARATION FOR BENCH REGULATION

For the purposes of this book we shall assume that the 'blow' (the distance between the nose of the hammer and the string) on your piano is $1\frac{7}{8}''$. There can, however, be slight variations so measure

GRAND ACTION BLOW

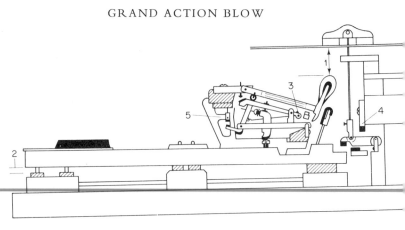

1. Hammer Blow $1\frac{7}{8}''$ from string.
2. Touch $\frac{3}{8}''$.
3. Repetition screw to spring.
4. Damper Stop Rail.
5. Set Off Escapement Dolly.

the blow in your piano by sliding your rule between the strings till the rule is touching the nose of the hammer. Measure the distance from the nose itself to the string.

Remove the action and the keys from piano and place on your bench. This bench must be flat and even. For bench regulation we need a length of wood, $57'' \times 2'' \times \frac{3}{4}''$, which will be known as the set off bar. On the ends of the set off bar, $1''$ in from the end and in the centre, you must fit a long bolt, protruding about $3''$ from the wood with a nut screwed onto the end of it.

To support this we need the following:

Two pieces of wood, $9\frac{3}{4}'' \times 2\frac{1}{2}'' \times 1\frac{3}{4}''$ and at the top end of both pieces a slot must be made, $\frac{1}{4}'' \times 3''$ deep, in the centre of each piece of wood. Next we screw these blocks to pieces of ply, $\frac{1}{4}'' \times 9''$ long $\times 1\frac{3}{4}''$ wide. The blocks must be at the extreme end of the ply, thus making an 'L' shape.

The purpose of this will become obvious. Placing the blocks at each end of the action, fit the set off bar in position—the bolt going between the long slots of your end pieces. Using your rule measure from the nose of the hammer in the treble $1\frac{7}{8}''$ to the under-neath of the set off bar, which should be in position over the hammers. Obviously any adjustment can be made by unscrewing the nut and lowering or raising the set off bar held in the slot by the bolt. Then tighten up the nut again.

We now deal with the first break note, i.e. the last hammer before the bass hammers which are longer. We will deal with the bass shortly. Therefore, from the first treble to the break hammer the measurement from the nose of the hammer to the set off bar above is $1\frac{7}{8}''$. The idea of this set off bar above the hammers, as you may have gathered, is to represent the strings and to enable you to do the bench regulation which is impossible inside the piano.

SET OFF

Depress the first treble key and the hammer will rise towards the set off bar above. If this blocks we must set this off $\frac{1}{8}''$ from the set off bar. This is done by turning down the escapement dolly. What

SET OFF BAR

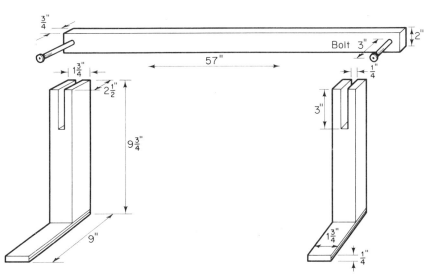

97

is actually happening when we turn down the escapement dolly is as follows:

When the key is depressed the lever rises up; the jack which is directly under the roller pushes up the hammer in turn; the hammer is travelling towards the string and when the hammer is $\frac{1}{8}''$ from the string, the dolly, at this point, should now touch the jack itself and the jack, which is pushing up the roller, is now withdrawn by the action of the dolly. The roller, losing the thrust of the jack, now drops onto the carriage. Thus the hammer drops into check.

Now go through all the notes in turn, making sure they set off $\frac{1}{8}''$ from the set off bar. Obviously if they set off too soon turn up the dollies to correct adjustment. This done we will now deal with the bass hammers. Raise the set off bar to $1\frac{7}{8}''$ and set off $\frac{1}{8}''$ as before.

On the hammer flange on a Grand we find the set off screw, the action of which is to work in conjunction with the escapement dolly. The actual function of this set off screw is as follows:

When the key is being depressed and the lever is rising, with the pressure of the set off screw on the rocker stop pad, this prevents the carriage rising higher at the same moment that the jack is withdrawn from the roller. The Grand set off screw hardly ever needs adjustment once it has been set by the original action finisher when the piano was newly made. There are exceptions, one being if, regardless of set off by the escapement dolly, the hammer still blocks. Turning the set off screw down carefully should remedy this. This set off screw may also be used if, after the hammer has set off, it still rides high on the carriage and does not drop into check. If the repetition spring is adjusted accurately (this will be dealt with shortly) by turning down the set off screw, this problem is usually cured effectively.

REGULATE REPETITION SPRINGS

Press down first key in treble in the usual way one would do when playing, the hammer striking the string and dropping back into check after setting off. Allow the finger still holding down the key to rise slowly. As the hammer is coming off check there should be a very slight movement or jump of the hammer from the check itself. This is caused by the jack going under the roller once again, by the strength of the spring. This is exactly what should happen, but if, after playing the note and your finger is slowly allowing the key to ride, instead of this slight jumping movement the hammer drops back immediately onto the hammer rest, one must strengthen the repetition spring. This is done by turning down the repetition screw slightly, giving extra strength to the spring. Try the note making sure it operates correctly as previously mentioned. If, on the other hand, after playing the note and the hammer is dropped into check, when the key is slowly allowed to rise the hammer jerks strongly, then the spring is too strong and should be

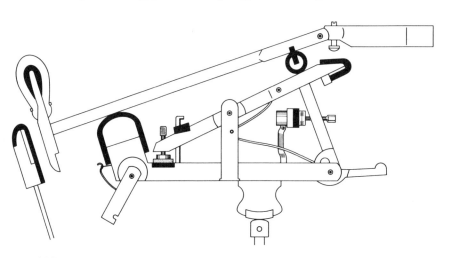

AN EXAMPLE OF AN OLDER TYPE OF GRAND ACTION

weakened by turning up the repetition screw until the spring has the correct strength.

In some pianos there is no screw for the spring adjustment. The spring is made in a slightly different way and there is no regulation screw at all. This spring has the appearance of a 'V'. The one length of the spring is inserted in the jack itself and is held in position on the lever. The top half of the spring from the spiral itself is fitted under the carriage in a groove. If the spring is too weak one has to bring the spring away from the groove under the carriage, bringing it to the side of the carriage and upwards and, carefully bending the spring up higher still, giving it extra bow, re insert spring in position in groove under carriage. The spring should now be strengthened. If, on the other hand, the spring is far too strong it will be weakened by slight pressure under the spring towards the underneath of the carriage.

Continue throughout the rest of the action, using whichever method is applicable.

ADJUSTMENT OF CHECKS AND TOUCH

Making sure that your set off bar is $1\frac{7}{8}''$ from the hammer nose, start from the first treble using your longer finger, index finger and thumb, and play the first three notes. These three hammers should have dropped into check after setting off. Hold these three hammers in this position. The distance of the nose of the hammer from the string, now the notes are in check, should be approximately $\frac{5}{8}''$. If the hammer is lower than this, release the hammers from check, lift up the hammer slightly, bend the check forwards towards you slightly, play the note and make sure the note is now approximately $\frac{5}{8}''$ from the string when in check. If the hammer drops into check closer to the string than $\frac{5}{8}''$, lift the hammer and bend the check slightly away from you. The idea of playing three notes at a time is to see that they follow the same line when in check. One need not use a rule to measure each note but use your eye to follow from the first note played. Whilst doing this one also deals with the touch. The touch of the naturals, when the note is depressed, should measure $\frac{3}{8}''$ deep. You should feel the hammer set off and a little drop afterwards. It is advisable to use a special touch weight, which will show you the depth of $\frac{3}{8}''$ correctly. If the touch is deeper than this, lift up the key, remove the front baize, insert a suitable thickness of card washer and replace the front baize on top of this. Try note once more. If the touch is too shallow, lift up key and remove the paper or card washers which are underneath the front baize (you will usually find in used pianos many card washers underneath the front baize). If the touch is too shallow and there are no card washers under the front baize, which can be removed, lift key and remove the front baize. Lay the baize on a piece of thick metal and with a heavy hammer, hammer the baize down slightly, to make the touch deep enough. Replace the front baize on the front pin and try the note once more.

Go throughout the piano in the same way. When this has all been completed, slide the action and keys once again into the piano, going through the same manoeuvre as mentioned before. The reason for this is to enable you to finally go through regulation once the action and keys are in the piano, as one sometimes finds slight differences between bench regulation and the final regulation in the piano. If, for example, during this last operation one finds that perhaps a hammer might not be setting off properly, one can set off whilst action and keys are in the piano.

All this completed, one now replaces key blocks, front and fall to piano.

786.23
K383p

66562

786.23
K303p

66562

Kennedy, K. T.
Piano action repairs
and maintenance

DATE DUE	BORROWER'S NAME	ROOM NUMBER

GAYLORD

PRINTED IN U.S.A.